NEWINGTON, CONNECTICUT

1880

Erik S. Hinckley

HERITAGE BOOKS
2021

HERITAGE BOOKS
AN IMPRINT OF HERITAGE BOOKS, INC.

Books, CDs, and more—Worldwide

For our listing of thousands of titles see our website
at
www.HeritageBooks.com

Published 2021 by
HERITAGE BOOKS, INC.
Publishing Division
5810 Ruatan Street
Berwyn Heights, Md. 20740

International Standard Book Number
Paperbound: 978-1-55613-047-2

Table of Contents

The importance of public records should not be overlooked when doing genealogy research. Here I have attempted to show the residents of Newington, Connecticut in 1880 (using a number of different sources to document and catalog them from that time). This work is an alphabetized listing of the residents which was derived from the 1880 census record for Newington. Since Newington had been a part of Wethersfield, Connecticut up until 1871, this is the first census of the people of Newington. The majority of the listed information is taken from that record. I hope to be able to create a "snapshot" in time for the Town of Newington to show the people and what they did during that time from the census and other local records.

Introduction to Sources

1880 Federal Census – The 1880 census for Newington was completed on June 1st and certified by census taker, Wm. E. Potter (a Newington resident), on 26-Jun-1880. There were 934 residents, 109 farms, 1 smith (blacksmith) and 2 manufacturers. To maintain continuity of the record I have used the dwelling number(s) and family number(s) as they appear on the census record. There are a number of instances where there is a break in the numbering of both dwelling and family numbers which in some cases leads to different families with the same dwelling or family number. Additionally, the spelling of names was taken directly from the census so some names may appear to be misspelled. In other cases given names were abbreviated as well. The individuals shown without a birth location were born in Connecticut per the census record. Occupations for women were typically listed as either "keeping house" or "at home." Those with different occupations were shown. Women shown as "keeping house" were usually the spouse of the head of household, or a single or widowed woman who was head of her own household. Single women aged 18 or older living in a household were typically noted as "at home." Typically children aged 10 or older attended school and are noted that way. I also reviewed the Special Schedule to the 1880 census which enumerated individuals described as "insane, idiotic or paupers." Those designated as "idiotic or insane" are marked as such on the regular census, paupers are not.

Deed References – All deed references were obtained from a search of the Newington land records which are available at the Town Clerk's office there. Some deeds contain multiple parcels of land as well as land in other towns. For clarification I have just given the acreages of the land in Newington (if noted in the deed). These deeds were all recorded in the year 1880. A number of these records are dated prior to 1880 but not recorded in Newington until that year. The deeds that were dated prior to 1871 were likely recorded in Wethersfield, as Newington was a part of that town until that year, prior to being recorded in Newington. I have listed the sales prices as they were recorded on the deeds. The volume and page listed for each document is for the Newington land records.

1880 Tax Levy – The original Tax Levy book was reviewed in the Newington Town Clerk's office In February 2020. The levy is as of 1-Oct-1880. It was certified by Chas. E. Chapman and Henry S. Kellogg on 15-Dec-1880. Most of the items that were assessed are self-explanatory. Livestock could be any of the following: horses, asses, mules or neat cattle. Typically neat cattle were horned oxen or young beef cattle, from which neatsfoot oil was produced (this term is obsolete today). The assessed prices for various heads of livestock ranged from $15 - $75 each, there wasn't a "standard" value for each type of animal. The same applies to houses and land, there appears to be no standard assessment value assigned for dwellings or acreage of land. Another item on the levy was titled "Money at interest in this State and Elsewhere," that would mean money in bank accounts or loans where interest was being earned. There is also an entry called: clocks, watches, timepieces, and jewelry, typically it wasn't designated as to which item it was, only a number. This also happens for the section noted as Piano Fortes or other musical instruments. Pianoforte is an older term no longer in use meaning a piano. Some individuals were also charged an additional 10% on their total assessment. It is unclear why this was done. Where that occurs I have noted the total includes the surcharge. Where land acreage is listed I have shown the total acreage and the breakdown (if listed) of the various parcels of land. There are individuals who lived outside of Newington that also appear on the levy. These people were likely former residents of the town, relatives of current residents or had business interests of some sort in Newington. Those individuals are listed in the Non-Resident Tax Levy section. There is also a separate entry that totals the entire Newington Tax Levy for 1880.

Burial Permits – were reviewed in the Newington Town Clerk's office between 2010 and 2015. I have chosen not to list the cause of death from these records. There are three cemeteries currently in Newington; West Meadow Cemetery, Church Street Cemetery, and the Newington Cemetery (a/k/a Center Cemetery). Many of the listed residents are buried in the Newington Cemetery or other burial grounds in surrounding towns. All of the burials listed on these permits are for the Church Street or Newington Cemeteries. I also used the Find A Grave website to verify headstone inscriptions as needed. In some cases burial permits were issued but no verified gravesite could be located. It's possible they could be un-marked graves or burials on private property. When a burial permit was issued and no headstone located, it is noted. Ages taken from these permits are typically listed as years-months-days, so in that case an age shown as 76-1-1 would be 76 years 1 month and 1 day.

Baptism and Marriage Records – were taken from the Roger Welles compilation (see bibliography). The marriages and baptisms noted all took place in the Congregational Church in Newington. The names, dates, locations, and spellings were taken verbatim from this record. In some cases the names on the census record differ from the baptism or marriage records, the varied spellings are noted as needed.

References to Town Meetings came directly from the minutes of those meetings that are archived in the Newington Town Clerk's office.

A sample entry looks like this:

Anderson, John (22) [the age in years of this person as listed on the census] was born in Sweden and worked as a farm laborer in the household of Walter F. Brown [the head of household where the individual resides on the census] (69, 76) [this pair of numbers indicates the dwelling # and family # where they reside on the census]. The census noted that he could neither read nor write.

Allenn, John (35) was married, born in Ireland and worked as a laborer in the household of Thomas Dennis (104, 111). The record does not show his wife residing with him. The census also notes that he could neither read nor write.

Anderson, John (22) was born in Sweden and worked as a farm laborer in the household of Walter F. Brown (69, 76). The census noted that he could neither read nor write.

Applebee, Abigail B. (73) resided with her husband M. Albert Applebee (74, 81). Abigail Whaples, of Wethersfield, Connecticut married Michael Applebee, of Middletown, Connecticut in Newington on 6-Mar-1826.

Applebee, M. Albert (75) was born in New York. He was married, worked as a blacksmith, and head of household (74, 81). Michael Applebee, of Middletown, Connecticut married Abigail Whaples, of Wethersfield, Connecticut on 6-Mar-1826 in Newington.

Applebee, Sarah E. (46) was born in Massachusetts and resided with her husband William Applebee (99, 106).

Applebee, William (52) was a married farmer and head of household (99, 106). There was a tax levy for Wm. L. Applebee that lists the following assets valued at $425: 1 house, ½ acre of land, and 2 head of livestock.

Applebee, William (9) lived with his parents, William and Sarah E., in household (99, 106). He was listed as their adopted son.

Atwood, Chas. K. (59) was head of household (50, 56). He was a single farmer and the brother of Josiah E. Atwood. A tax levy valued at $3,997 was in the name of the C.K. Atwood & Co. That assessment included: ¾ of a house, 82 acres of land, 10 head of livestock, and poultry. The property was noted as follows: Old Home Lot – 11 ac, White Brick – 25 ac, Meadow – 9 ac, Chester – 23 ac, and Webster – 14 ac. C.K. Atwood served as moderator for the town meetings of 14-Jun-1880 and 18-Oct-1880. He was also elected as a School Visitor at the 4-Oct-1880 meeting and at the 18-Oct-1880 meeting was appointed by the selectmen as a Deputy Registrar of Voters. Charles was elected to serve as a Justice of the Peace at the 8-Nov-1880 meeting. Charles Kellogg Atwood, son of Josiah and Prudence, was baptized in Newington on 5-Aug-1821 and later died in Hartford, Connecticut on 18-Sep-1912, aged 91-8-25. He is buried in the Newington Cemetery.

Atwood, Elbert W. (11) attended school and lived with his parents, Josiah E. and Jerusha E. in household (49, 55). He is buried in the Newington Cemetery with his parents, the Atwood headstone lists him as; Their Son / Elbert W. Atwood / 1868 – 1953.

Atwood, Isabel E. (14) attended school and lived with her parents, Josiah E. and Jerusha E. in household (49, 55). Isabel Ellis Atwood was baptized in Newington on 1-Nov-1866.

Atwood, Jerusha E. (54) resided with her children and husband Josiah E. (49, 55). Jerusha Ellis Atwood died in Newington on 29-May-1903 at the age of 76-11-28. She is buried with her husband in the Newington Cemetery, and is listed on the Atwood headstone as; Jerusha Ellis / His Wife / 1826 – 1908.

Atwood, Josiah E. (57) was head of household (49, 55). He was a married farmer and brother of Chas. K. Atwood. J.E. Atwood had a tax levy valued at $2,069 which included: 1 house, 41 ½ acres of land, and 7 head of livestock. The property was known as: Home Lot – 14 ac, Boardman – 3 ½ ac, Webster – 10 ac, and Bush – 14 ac. He was elected as a Highway Surveyor at the 4-Oct-1880 town meeting. Josiah Elbert Atwood, son of Josiah and Prudence, was baptized in Newington on 6-Jul-1823. He is buried in the Newington Cemetery, the Atwood headstone lists him as; Josiah E. Atwood / 1823 – 1898.

Atwood, Julia N. (48) was single and resided with her brother Chas. K. Atwood (50, 56). Julia Norton Atwood, daughter of Josiah and Prudence, was baptized in Newington on 10-Jun-1832. Julia is buried in the Newington cemetery, the dates on her headstone are mostly illegible. The Hale collection information lists her birth as 5-Sep-1831 and death as 5-Dec-1908.

Atwood, Kate M. (19) was a single school teacher who resided with her parents Josiah E. and Jerusha E. (49, 55). She was baptized Kate Mary Atwood on 21-Jul-1861 in Newington. Mary Atwood Francis died on 23-Nov-1946 in Westmoreland, New Hampshire aged 86-2-13. She is buried in the Newington cemetery with her husband, Arlan P. Francis (52, 58) and is shown on the Francis headstone as; Kate M. Atwood His Wife / Sep. 10, 1860 – Nov. 25, 1946. There appears to be a slight discrepancy for the date of death between the burial permit and headstone.

Atwood, Mary K. (50) was single and resided with her brother Chas. K. Atwood (50, 56). Mary Kellogg Atwood, daughter of Josiah and Prudence, was baptized in Newington on 13-Jun-1830. She was the second wife of John S. Kirkham (94, 101). Mary K. Kirkham died in Newington on 22-Sep-1919 and is buried with John in the Newington Cemetery. The Kirkham headstone lists her as; Mary K. Atwood / Wife Of / John S. Kirkham / Feb. 26, 1830 / Sept. 22, 1919.

Atwood, Thos. R. (55) was a single farmer who lived with his brother Chas. K. Atwood (50, 56). Thomas Robbins Atwood, son of Josiah and Prudence, was baptized in Newington on 24-Oct-1824 and died there on 12-Jan-1904 at the age of 79-6-22. Thomas was elected as a Registrar of Voters at the 4-Oct-1880 town meeting. He is buried in the Newington Cemetery and shown on the Atwood stone as; Thomas R. Atwood / June 20, 1824 / Jan. 12, 1904.

Bacon, Maria A. (46) was a single house keeper who worked in the household of Elias L. Steele (153, 161).

Bader, Anna (12) lived with her siblings and parents Jacob and Charlotte (136, 142).

Bader, Charlotte (35) was born in Germany and resided with her children and husband Jacob Bader (136, 142). She is buried in the Spring Grove Cemetery in Hartford, Connecticut with Jacob. The Hale collection record lists her birth as 1-Jul-1844 and death as 20-Jan-1901.

Bader, Ernest (8) lived with his siblings and parents, Jacob and Charlotte (136, 142). He is buried in the Spring Grove Cemetery in Hartford, Connecticut. The stone shows him as; Ernest Bader / 1872 – 1916.

Bader, Hattie (5) lived with her siblings and parents Jacob and Charlotte (136, 142).

Bader, Jacob (38) was born in Germany, married and worked as a stone mason. He was head of household (136, 142). The tax levy for Jacob listed assets valued at $1,110 which included: 1 house, 6 acres of land, and 6 head of livestock. He is buried with his wife Charlotte in the Spring Grove Cemetery in Hartford, Connecticut. The Hale collection lists his birth as 14-Dec-1842 and death as 31-Oct-1898.

Bader, Katie (10) lived with her siblings and parents Jacob and Charlotte (136, 142). According to the 18-Feb-1907 Hartford Courant, "Mrs. Kate KOSETZKE of No. 330 Park Street, died late last night at St. Francis's Hospital, where she had been but a few hours. She was 35 years old". She is buried in the Spring Grove Cemetery in Hartford, Connecticut.

Bader, Minnie (2) lived with her siblings and parents Jacob and Charlotte (136, 142). Minnie E. Bader died on 15-Oct-1881 aged 3 y. 11 m. and is buried in the Newington cemetery.

Bankson, Pere (27) was single and born in Sweden. He worked as a laborer in the household of Thomas Dennis (104, 111). He could not read or write.

Banta, Garrett (24) was a single farm laborer who worked in the household of Chas. K. Atwood (50, 56).

Banta, George (23) was born in New Jersey, single, and worked as a farm laborer in the household of John S. Kirkham (94, 101).

Barnard, Ada (25) was single and resided with her parents, Horace and Harriet, in household (146, 152). She died in Newington on 24-Jan-1933 at the age of 77-9-7. A burial permit was filed in Newington but no documented gravesite has been located.

Barnard, Edward R. (12) lived with his parents, Horace and Harriet, in household (146, 152). Edward Raymond Barnard died in Canton, Connecticut on 31-Jan-1939 at the age of 70 y. 8 m. A burial permit was filed in Newington but no documented gravesite has been located.

Barnard, Grace (18) was single and resided with her parents Horace and Harriet in household (146, 152).

Barnard, Harriet (57) resided with her husband Horace Barnard (146, 152).

Barnard, Horace (59) was a married farmer and head of household (146, 152). The tax levy for Horace listed a total value of $4,459. The levy included: 1 house, 156 acres of land, and 9 head of livestock. The property was described as follows: Home Lot – 115 ac, West Lot – 33 ac, and Buck – 8 ac. His headstone in the Newington Cemetery reads; Horace Barnard / Died / March 5, 1891 / Aged 70.

Barrett, James (45) was a single farm laborer from Ireland, who worked in the household of Franklin C. Latimer (168, 176).

Baxter, Harriet (47) was born in Massachusetts and resided with her son and husband, James Baxter (114, 121). She is possibly buried in Ellington, Connecticut (see James Baxter).

Baxter, James (47) was a married farmer born in Vermont who was head of household (114, 121). The tax levy for Mr. Baxter was $110 (surcharge) for 3 head of livestock. James was elected as a Grand Juror at the 4-Oct-1880 town meeting. There is a James Baxter buried with his wife and 3 other children in the Ellington Center Cemetery in Ellington, Connecticut, the dates appear to be a good match for both James and Harriet.

Baxter, William H. (13) lived with his parents James and Harriet in household (114, 121). He is possibly buried in Ellington, Connecticut (see James Baxter).

Beck, Henry (26) was single, born in Germany, and worked as a farm laborer in the household of Henry Fields (151, 159). He is possibly buried in the Spring Grove Cemetery in Hartford, Connecticut. That individual died on 5-Dec-1901 at the age of 47 y.

Beeman, Allan (20) was a single, black laborer from North Carolina. He worked in the household of R. Wells Kellogg (56, 62). It's likely he was to be related to Cornelius Beeman.

Beeman, Cornelius (20) was a single, black laborer from North Carolina. He worked in the household of R. Wells Kellogg (56, 62). It would appear that he was related to Allan Beeman.

Belden, Agnes W. (33) was single and resided with her brother Joshua Belden (70, 77). Agnes Whittlesey Belden, daughter of John M. and Mary E.H., was baptized on 4-Jul-1847 in Newington and later died there on 23-Feb-1921 at the age of 74-1-5. The Belden headstone in the Newington Cemetery lists her as; Children of J.M. & M.E.H. Belden / Agnes W. / Jan. 18, 1847 / Feb. 23, 1921.

Belden, Cornelia H. (35) was single and resided with her brother Joshua Belden (70, 77). She was baptized, Cornelia Hale Belden, daughter of John M. and Mary E.H., on 20-Jul-1845 in Newington and is buried there in the Newington Cemetery. The Belden headstone shows her as; Children Of / J.M. & M.E.H. Belden / Cornelia H. / April 11, 1845 / April 19, 1881.

Belden, Fanny H. (27) resided with her mother, extended family, and husband Joshua Belden (70, 77).

Belden, Joshua (31) was a married farmer and head of household (70, 77). His tax levy is valued at $55 (surcharge) for 1 clock/watch. There was also a levy for the estate of J.M. Belden (John M. Belden was Joshua's father) which was valued at $13,522.89. Items on that assessment included: 1 house, 129 acres of land, 17 head of livestock, 3 coaches/carriages, $5,540 in bank and insurance stock, money at interest of $50, and $133.89 cash on hand. The property of the estate was noted as: Home Lot – 78 ac, Wells – 37 ac, Mountain – 7 ac, and Brace – 7 ac. Joshua was appointed as a Juror by the Town Selectmen at the 5-Jan-1880 town meeting. He was also elected as a Highway Surveyor at the 4-Oct-1880 meeting. Joshua, son of John M. and Mary E.H., was baptized in Newington on 1-Apr-1849 and died in Hartford, Connecticut on 20-Sep-1924 at the age of 70 y. He is buried in the Newington Cemetery, the Belden Headstone shows him as; Joshua Belden / Dec. 14, 1848 / Sept. 20, 1924.

Belden, Julia M. (27) was single and resided with her brother Joshua (70, 77). Julia, daughter of John M. and Mary E.H., was baptized in Newington on 5-Jun-1853. Julia Mason Belden died in Newington on 26-Dec-1923 at the age of 71-0-9 and is buried with her family members in the Newington Cemetery. The Belden stone lists her as; Children Of / J.M. & M.E.H. Belden / Julia M. / Dec. 17, 1852 / Dec. 26, 1923.

Belden, Mary E. (40) was another single sister who also resided with her brother Joshua (70, 77). Mary Elizabeth Belden, daughter of John M. and Mary E.H., was baptized in Newington on 9-Feb-1840 and died there on 17-Jan-1913 at the age of 73-4-9. She is buried with other family members in the Newington Cemetery, the Belden family stone lists her as; Children Of / J.M. & M.E.H. Belden / Mary E. / Sept. 8, 1839 / Jan. 17, 1913.

Belden, Mary H. (68) was a widow who resided with her son Joshua (70, 77). It appears that she had her own tax levy valued at $3,432. Items listed included: 76 ½ acres of land known as the Hale Farm, 1 piano, $918 in bank and insurance stock, and $144 money at interest. She is buried in the Newington Cemetery with her husband, John Mason Belden, the headstone shows her as, Mary E. Hale / His Wife / Born Mar. 16, 1812 / Died Feb. 3, 1888.

Benson, Daniel B. (42) was a married farmer and head of household (147, 153). His tax levy was valued at $450 which included: 1 house, 14 acres of land, and 2 head of livestock. There is a Daniel B. Benson buried in the Wethersfield Village Cemetery in Wethersfield, Connecticut which could be the same person. That burial lists dates born in 1839 and died in 1898.

Benson, Harriet (51) resided with her husband Daniel B. Benson (147, 153).

Blinn, Albert (6) lived with his siblings and parents, Walter U. and Sarah M. Blinn (67, 74).

Blinn, Charles (21) was a single farm laborer that resided with his widowed mother Sarah Blinn (128, 135).

Blinn, Edward (11) attended school that year and lived with his siblings and parents Walter U. and Sarah M. Blinn (67, 74). There is an Edward W. Blinn 1868 – 1942 buried in the Newington Cemetery, this could be the same individual.

Blinn, Emily (13) attended school and lived with her siblings and widowed mother Sarah Blinn (128, 135).

Blinn, George (14) attended school that year and lived with his siblings and parents Walter U. and Sarah M. (67, 74). George B. Blinn died in Newington, on 21-Feb-1931, at the age of 65-8-25 and is buried in the Newington Cemetery. His headstone reads; George B. Blinn / 1867 – 1931.

Blinn, Henry (52) was a widowed farm laborer who resided with his mother Sarah Blinn (128, 135). The census also indicates that he could neither read nor write. A tax levy for Henry W. Blinn lists a total value of $209 (surcharge) for the following items: 1 house and 2 head of livestock. Henry W. Blinn, of Wethersfield, Connecticut married Harriet Redfield, of Killingworth, Connecticut, in Newington on 25-Mar-1857.

Blinn, Porter (16) was a single farm laborer who lived with his widowed mother Sarah Blinn (128, 135).

Blinn, Riley (12) attended school and lived with his siblings and parents Walter U. & Sarah M. (67, 74).

Blinn, Sarah M. (36) resided with her husband Walter U. Blinn (67, 74).

Blinn, Sarah (7) lived with her parents Walter U. & Sarah M. (67, 74).

Blinn, Sarah (71) was a widow who resided with her children and was head of household (128, 135).

Blinn, Walter U. (38) was a married farmer and head of household (67, 74).

Blinn, Wells (41) was a single farm laborer who resided with his widowed mother Sarah Blinn (128, 135). According to the census he could neither read nor write.

Blinn, Wells (15) was a farm laborer who worked in the household of Henry Luce (167, 175).

Blinn, William (18) was a single farm laborer who resided with his widowed mother Sarah Blinn (128, 135).

Blodgett, Ralph (35) was a divorced farm laborer who worked in the household of Walter F. Brown (69, 76).

Boardman, Carrie (9) lived with her parents John H. and Sarah H. Boardman (9, 12).

Boardman, John H. (42) was a married farm laborer and head of household (9, 12). The tax levy for John had assets valued at $1,700. Those items included: 1 house, 20 acres of land, and 3 head of livestock. He married Sarah H. Dix on 18-Apr-1867 in Newington. John is buried in the Fairview Cemetery in New Britain, Connecticut, the Boardman headstone lists him as; John H. Boardman / 1836 – 1910.

Boardman, Nathaniel (82) was born in New York, widowed and resided with his son William Boardman (34, 40).

Boardman, Sarah H. (39) resided with her husband John H. Boardman (9, 12). Sarah H. Dix married John H. Boardman, of New Britain, Connecticut in Newington on 18-Apr-1867. She is buried in the Fairview Cemetery in New Britain, Connecticut, with her husband. The Boardman headstone lists her as; Sarah H. Dix / His Wife / 1840-1898.

Boardman, William (38) was a farm laborer who resided with his sister and was head of household (34, 40).

Bogardus, Adelbert (16) was a farm laborer from New York who worked in the household of Marcus L. Stoddard (20, 26).

Boynton family (178, 186). This family is clearly enumerated as Boynton in the census record; however, other vital records for this family use the spelling of Boyington. To maintain continuity I shall use the census record spelling and indicate other records where the spelling changes.

Boynton, Alfred (33) was married, worked as a joiner, and was head of household (178, 186). Alfred Ensign Boyington died in Newington on 1-Jan-1918 at the age of 71-6-24. He is buried in the Newington Cemetery and his stone reads; Alfred E. Boyington / Born June 6, 1846 / Died Jan. 1, 1918.

Boynton, Charles (1) lived with his siblings and parents Alfred and Oresvilla (178, 186). He is buried in the Newington Cemetery with his wife Cora, their headstone reads; Boyington / Charles Lucius / 1879 – 1953.

Boynton, Herbert (6) lived with his siblings and parents Alfred and Oresvilla (178, 186). He is buried with his wife, Ethel, in the Mountain View Cemetery in Bloomfield, Connecticut, their headstone reads; Herbert A. / Boyington / 1874 – 1939.

Boynton, Ida (3) lived with her siblings and parents Alfred and Oresvilla (178, 186).

Boynton, Lottie (4) lived with her siblings and parents Alfred and Oresvilla (178, 186).

Boynton, Oresvilla (27) resided with her children and husband Alfred Boynton (178, 186). Oresvilla Elenora Boyington died in Hartford, Connecticut, aged 90-11-19, on 24-Apr-1944. She is buried in the Newington Cemetery, the stone reads; Orsevilla E. Burdict / Wife Of / Alfred E. Boyington / 1853 – 1944.

Braman, Caroline (63) was a widow who resided with her son-in-law John H. Fish (13, 16). A tax levy exists for Mrs. Milton Braman [Milton died in 1878] for $1,200. The only item listed was a house. She is buried with her husband in the North Cemetery in West Hartford, Connecticut. The Braman headstone lists her as; Caroline His Wife / Died Oct. 26, 1888 AE 72.

Brany, Rosa (19) was a single servant who worked in the household of Hannah L. Whittlesey (115, 122).

Brown, Abigail K. (65) was single and resided with her brother Walter F. Brown (69, 76). Abigail was also listed on the Supplemental Schedule for the 1880 census and was shown in the insane section with the disease of Melancholia. She is buried in the Newington Cemetery with other family members, the Brown family headstone shows her as; Abigail K. Died Aug. 21, 1881 / Aged 68.

Brown, Elizabeth S. (62) resided with her husband Walter F. Brown (69, 76). Elizabeth Seymour, of Wethersfield, Connecticut married Walter F. Brown, also of Wethersfield, on 29-Apr-1863 in Newington. She is buried with her husband and other Brown family members in the Newington Cemetery. The Brown family headstone lists her as; Elizabeth S. His Wife / Born Feb. 13, 1818 / Died May 24, 1893.

Brown, Rhoda (73) was a single housekeeper who worked in the household of R. Wells Kellogg (56, 62). The Brown headstone in the Newington Cemetery shows her as; Children of Lyman & Sarah Brown / Rhoda / Born May 17, 1808 / Died Apr. 9, 1896.

Brown, Sarah A. (62) was single and resided with her brother William F. Brown (69, 76). She is buried with other family members in the Newington Cemetery. The Brown family headstone lists her as; Sarah A. Died July 14, 1881 / Aged 64.

Brown, Walter F. (60) was a married farmer and head of household (69, 76). His tax levy was valued at $14,240 which included: 3 houses, 142 acres of land, 18 head of livestock, $5,520 in bank stock, and $100 money at interest. The property was known as: House Lot – 42 ac, West Lot – 5 ac, Whittlesey – 53 ac, South – 5 ac, Gladding – 26 ac, Parsonage – 4 ac, and Seymour – 7 ac. He married Elizabeth Seymour, of Wethersfield, Connecticut on 29-Apr-1863 in Newington. The Brown family headstone in the Newington Cemetery lists him as; Walter F. Brown / Born Mar. 5, 1820 / Died Nov. 26, 1885.

Burke, Henry (38) was a single farm laborer who worked in the household of John Webster (159, 167).

Burt, Frank M. (29) was born in Massachusetts, single, and worked as a Toy Cap Manufacturer. He was also head of household (32, 38). The Hale Collection notes a Frank G. Burt 1851 – 1920 is buried in the Grove Cemetery in Windsor Locks, Connecticut. This may be the same person.

Burt, James C. (27) was single and from Massachusetts. He worked and lived with his brother Frank M. Burt (32, 38).

Byrne, Catherine (52) was a widow born in Ireland and head of household (126, 133). Her tax levy was for $1,292 (surcharge) which included: 1 house, 20 ½ acres of land, and 6 head of livestock.

Byrne, Elizabeth (30) resided with her children and husband Peter Byrne (129, 136). The Hale Collection notes Elizabeth M. Welch Byrne, wife of Peter M, 1849 – 1914, is buried in the Mount Saint Benedict Cemetery in Bloomfield, Connecticut.

Byrne, Jennie E. (14) lived with her sisters and mother, Catherine Byrne (126, 133).

Byrne, Julia A. (26) was single and resided with her sisters and mother, Catherine Byrne (126, 133).

Byrne, Kittie (2) lived with her siblings and parents Peter and Elizabeth (129, 136).

Byrne, Lucy M. (20) was single and resided with her sisters and mother, Catherine Byrne (126, 133).

Byrne, Mary (5) lived with her siblings and parents Peter and Elizabeth (129, 136).

Byrne, Peter (31) was born in Ireland, worked as a milkman, and was head of household (129, 136). The tax levy for Peter was valued at $566 (surcharge) which included: 1 house, 1 acre of land, and 3 head of livestock. The Hale Collection notes Peter M. Byrne, 1848 – 1917 is buried in the Mount Saint Benedict Cemetery in Bloomfield, Connecticut.

Cahill, Patrick (28) was single, born in Ireland and worked as a farm laborer in the household of Lester Luce (166, 174). There is a Patrick Cahill, 1852 – 1892, buried in the St. John's Cemetery in Middletown, Connecticut that could be this individual.

Callahan, Catherine A. (27) resided with her son and husband James Callahan (131, 137).

Callahan, Elizabeth (31) resided with her children and husband James Callahan (130, 136).

Callahan, Henrietta M. (3) lived with her parents James and Elizabeth (130, 136).

Callahan, James E. (5) lived with his parents James and Catherine A. (131, 137).

Callahan, James (31) was a married farmer who was head of household (130, 136).

Callahan, James (31) was a married farmer and head of household (131, 137).

Callahan, Matthew (80) was born in Ireland, widowed and resided with his son James Callahan (131, 137). The tax levy for Matthew was valued at $1,237 (surcharge) which included: 1 house and 37 acres of land. The Hale Collection lists a Matthew Callahan, d. 12-Jan-1887, age 87 as being buried in the Cedar Hill Cemetery in Hartford, Connecticut. This could be the same person.

Callahan, William J. (9) lived with his siblings and parents James and Elizabeth in household (130, 136).

Camp, Augusta L. (14) lived with her siblings and parents Joseph and Eliza A. in household (43, 49). The Camp family headstone in the Newington Cemetery lists her as; Children Of / Joseph & Eliza Camp / 1865 Augusta L. 1905.

Camp, Chas. E. (3) lived with his parents Joseph and Eliza A. (43, 49).

Camp, Delia W. (71) was a widow who resided with her son Lemuel Camp (117, 124). A joint tax levy existed in the names of D.W. and L.W. [likely her son Lemuel W.] Camp for $16,027 (surcharge) which included the following: 2 houses, 144 acres of land, 18 head of livestock, 3 coaches, 3 clocks, 2 pianos, $2,606 in bank and insurance stock, $3,280 money at interest and $150 cash on hand. The property was noted as: Home Lot – 82 ac, Hurlbut – 30 ac, Brush Hill – 13 ac, Chester – 1 ac, and Kellogg – 18 ac. Delia Whittlesey, of Wethersfield, Connecticut married Homer Camp, of Washington, Connecticut in Newington on 19-Nov-1828. The Camp family headstone in the Newington Cemetery lists her as; His Wife / Delia Whittlesey / Born Aug. 1, 1808 / Died Oct. 21, 1894.

Camp, Eliza A. (39) resided with her children and husband Joseph Camp (43, 49). She is buried in the Newington Cemetery with her husband, the Camp stone lists her as; Eliza Ann Holcomb / His Wife / 1840 – 1916.

Camp, Geo. B. (9) lived with his siblings and parents Joseph and Eliza (43, 49). There is a George B. Camp buried in the Evergreen Cemetery in Gainesville, Florida. The headstone lists dates as 3-Apr-1871 and 11-Oct-1944 and his wife as Ellen P. Camp. This could be the same person.

Camp, John P. (5) lived with his siblings and parents Joseph and Eliza (43, 49). The Camp stone in the Newington Cemetery lists him as; Children Of / Joseph & Eliza Camp / 1875 John P. 1901.

Camp, Jos. W. (17) attended school that year and lived with his siblings and parents Joseph and Eliza (43, 49). Joseph W. Camp died in Preston, Connecticut on 19-May-1947 aged 83-6-18. He is listed on the Camp family headstone in the Newington Cemetery and shown as; Children Of / Joseph & Eliza Camp / 1862 Joseph W. 1947.

Camp, Joseph (46) was a farmer who lived with his wife and children. He was head of household (43, 49). The tax levy for Joseph was valued as $2,681 (there appears to be an addition error in the record as the total is actually $2,691). Items on the assessment included: 1 house, 48 ¾ acres of land, and 10 head of livestock. The property was listed as: Home Lot – 4 ac, Flagg – 13 ac, and Common – 31 ¾ ac. The Camp family headstone in the Newington Cemetery shows him as; Joseph Camp / 1834 – 1914.

Camp, Katie (16) was in school that year and lived with her siblings, father Lemuel and stepmother Mary (117, 124).

Camp, Laura (14) attended school that year and lived with her siblings, father Lemuel and stepmother Mary (117, 124). Laura Camp, daughter of Lemuel W. and Eliza, was baptized in Newington on 4-Jan-1867. Laura Kellogg Camp died on 17-Nov-1941 at the age of 76-2-5 and is buried in the Newington Cemetery with her sisters. The Camp headstone reads; Daughters Of / L.W. And Eliza Camp / Laura K. / Born Sept. 12, 1865 / Died Nov. 17, 1941.

Camp, Lemuel W. (50) was a married farmer and head of household (117, 124). A joint tax levy existed in the names of D.W. [likely his mother Delia W.] and L.W. Camp for $16,027 (surcharge) which included the following: 2 houses, 144 acres of land, 18 head of livestock, 3 coaches, 3 clocks, 2 pianos, $2,606 in bank and insurance stock, $3,280 in money at interest and $150 cash on hand. The property was noted as: Home Lot – 82 ac, Hurlbut – 30 ac, Brush Hill – 13 ac, Chester – 1 ac, and Kellogg – 18ac. There is another tax levy for L.W. Camp, as Trustee, valued at $2,800 for money at interest. Lemuel Whittlesey Camp, son of Homer and Delia, was baptized in Newington on 20-Jun-1830. He is buried in the Newington Cemetery with his family. His headstone reads; Lemuel W. Camp / Born Nov. 6, 1829 / Died Oct. 30, 1906.

Camp, Lizzie W. (19) resided with her siblings, father Lemuel, and stepmother Mary (117, 124). Eliza Webster Camp, daughter of Lemuel and Eliza, was baptized in Newington on 31-Oct-1861. The Camp family headstone, in the Newington Cemetery, reads; Daughters Of / L.W. And Eliza Camp / Eliza W. / Born Feb. 3, 1861 / Died Sept. 20, 1892.

Camp, Mary R. (45) resided with her daughter, stepchildren and husband Lemuel W. Camp (117, 124). Mary Robbins, daughter of Unni and Sarah Robbins, was baptized on 18-Oct-1835 in Newington. The Camp family headstone, in the Newington Cemetery reads as follows; Mary Robbins / Wife Of / L.W. Camp / Born Apr. 2, 1835 / Died Mar. 27, 1892.

Camp, Mary R. (4) lived with her half-siblings and parents Lemuel W. and Mary R. (117, 124). She is buried in the Newington Cemetery with her parents, the stone reads; Their Daughter / Mary R. Camp / Born Jan. 30, 1876 / Died Oct. 22, 1954.

Camp, Norman P. (12) went to school that year and lived with his siblings and parents, Joseph and Eliza (43, 49). He is buried in Newington Cemetery the headstone reads; Norman P. Camp / May 27, 1868 / Feb. 24, 1951.

Canfield, Addie L. (6) lived with her siblings and parents, Preston and Mary A. (31, 37).

Canfield, Lucian H. (12) attended school that year and resided with his siblings and parents, Preston and Mary A. (31, 37). The headstone in the Newington Cemetery reads; Lucia H. / Daughter Of / Preston & Mary A. / Canfield / Died Apr. 30, 1892 / Aged 24 Yrs. It appears that there may have been an error on the census record as Lucian H. is noted as a male, however the headstone shows Lucia as a daughter.

Canfield, Mary A. (36) resided with her children and husband, Preston Canfield (31, 37). She died in Wethersfield, Connecticut on 4-Mar-1924 at the age of 79-10-5. Her headstone in the Newington Cemetery shows, Mary Heath / wife of / Preston Canfield / 1844 – 1924.

Canfield, Merrill N. (1) lived with his siblings and parents, Preston and Mary A. (31, 37).

Canfield, Preston (38) was married, worked as a polisher and was head of household (31, 37). He died in Hartford, Connecticut on 17-Jun-1921 at the age of 76 y. His headstone in the Newington Cemetery reads; Preston Canfield / 1842 – 1921.

Canfield, Walter J. (8) lived with his siblings and parents, Preston and Mary A. (31, 37). Walter Joshua Canfield died in Newington on 21-Oct-1943 at the age of 72-0-10. The Canfield headstone in the Newington Cemetery lists him as; 1871 Walter J. 1943.

Capron, Carroll (20) was born in New Hampshire, single, and worked as a farm laborer in the household of Lester Luce (166, 174).

Carter, Jerusha (94) was a widow who resided with her son William Carter (111, 118).

Carter, Nancy W. (67) resided with her husband William Carter (111, 118).

Carter, William (65) was a farmer and head of household (111, 118). The tax levy was for Wm. Carter and was valued at $225 for 1 house and 1 head of livestock. William was appointed as a Juror by the Town Selectmen at the 5-Jan-1880 town meeting.

Carty, Patrick (24) was born in Ireland, single, and worked as a farm laborer in the household of Chas. J. Wells (119, 126).

Chapman, Charles E. (42) was a married farmer and head of household (169, 177). The tax levy was for Chas. E. Chapman and valued at $1,649 (which included an abatement of $100). Items included on the assessment were: 1 house, 47 acres of land, and 10 head of livestock. The property was identified as: Home Lot – 18 ac and Kelsey Lot – 29 ac. At the town meeting of 4-Oct-1880 Charles was elected as an Assessor.

Chapman, Elmer E. (16) attended school that year and lived with his siblings and parents, Charles E. and Mary J. (169, 177).

Chapman, Harriet (45) was born in England and resided with her husband John Chapman (97, 104).

Chapman, Henry H. (14) attended school that year and lived with his siblings and parents, Charles E. and Mary J. (169, 177).

Chapman, John (45) was born in England and worked as a machinist. He was head of household (97, 104). His tax levy was valued at $900 which included: 1 house, 11 acres of land, and 1 head of livestock.

Chapman, Marion (10) she was in school that year and lived with her siblings and parents, Charles E. and Mary J. (169, 177).

Chapman, Mary A. (63) was a widow and resided with her son Charles E. Chapman (169, 177).

Chapman, Mary J. (45) resided with her children and husband Charles E. Chapman (169, 177).

Chidley, Carrie R. (10) attended school that year and lived with her siblings and parents, Geo. E. and Sarah E. (22, 28).

Chidley, Geo. E. (41) was born in Massachusetts, worked as a Machinist, and was head of household (22, 28). The tax levy for M. Chidley was valued at $660 (surcharge) which included: 1 house and 2 head of livestock. At the town meeting of 4-Oct-1880, George was elected as a Constable and later as a Justice of the Peace at the 8-Nov-1880 meeting. He is buried in the Spring Grove Cemetery in Hartford, Connecticut his headstone reads; George E. Chidley / 1838 – 1923.

Chidley, Jennie E. (12) was in school, and lived with her siblings and parents, Geo. E. and Sarah E. (22, 28).

Chidley, Sarah E. (41) resided with her children and husband Geo. E. Chidley (22, 28). Sarah is buried with her husband in the Spring Grove Cemetery in Hartford, Connecticut her headstone reads; Sarah E. Hoxie / his wife / 1835 – 1911.

Christiansen, Dora (29) was born in Germany and resided with her children and, husband Peter (27, 33). She is buried in the North Cemetery in West Hartford, Connecticut with her husband and son. The headstone shows her as Dorothea 1846 – 1932.

Christiansen, Fred (2) was born in Vermont and lived with his sister and parents, Peter and Dora (27, 33). He is buried with his parents in the North Cemetery in West Hartford, Connecticut. The headstone shows him as; Frederick C. / son of / Peter & Dorothea / Died Nov. 18, 1888 / Aged 11 yrs. He is also listed on a separate Christiansen family headstone with his parents.

Christiansen, Jessie (4) she was born in Vermont and lived with her brother and parents, Peter and Dora (27, 33).

Christiansen, Peter (29) was born in Germany, married and worked as a laborer. He was also head of household (27, 33). Peter is buried in the North Cemetery in West Hartford, Connecticut with his wife and son Frederick. The Christiansen family headstone shows his dates as 1843 – 1908.

Churchill, Ellen A. (23) was single and resided with her siblings and parents, William and Sarah (150, 156).

Churchill, George E. (21) was a single farm laborer who resided with his brother and parents, Samuel S. and Louisa (132, 138). George Edward Churchill died in Newington on 11-Jul-1931 at the age of 72-7. His headstone in the Newington Cemetery reads; Churchill / George E. / 1858 – 1931.

Churchill, Henry D. (30) was a single school teacher who resided with his brother and parents, Samuel S. and Louisa (132, 138).

Churchill, Henry L. (17) was a farm laborer who lived with his siblings and parents, William and Sarah (150, 156).

Churchill, Joseph B. (19) was a single farm laborer who resided with his siblings and parents, William and Sarah (150, 156). It's possible he died in 1934 and is buried in New York.

Churchill, Louisa (54) resided with her children and husband Samuel S. Churchill (132, 138). She is buried with her husband and listed on a Churchill headstone in the Newington Cemetery as; Louisa A. His Wife / 1825 – 1894.

Churchill, Lucy (79) was a widow, who lived alone, and was head of household (142, 148). The tax levy for Lucy was valued at $780 which included: 1 house, 20 acres of land, and money at interest of $100. She is buried in the Newington Cemetery and her headstone reads; Aunt Lucy / Lucy Churchill / Died / Mar. 30, 1883 / AE 83.

Churchill, Mary (43) was single, lived alone, and head of household (154, 162). Her tax levy totaled $860 which included: 1 house, 20 acres of land, and 3 head of livestock. Mary died in Newington on 8-Jun-1930 aged 93-7-10 and is buried in the Newington Cemetery with her parents. The Churchill stone lists her as; Mary Churchill / Died / June 8, 1930 / AE 83. There appears to an age discrepancy between the burial permit and headstone.

Churchill, Samuel S. (55) was a married farmer and head of household (132, 138). The tax levy for Samuel was valued at $1,397 and included: 1 house, 36 acres of land, 9 head of livestock, and 15 sheep. The property was identified as: Home Lot – 6 ac, East – 6 ac, Webster – 10 ac, Robbins – 3 ½ ac, Standish – 6 ac, and Wood – 4 ½ ac. He is buried in the Newington Cemetery with his wife and parents. The headstone lists him as; Samuel S. Churchill / 1825 – 1900.

Churchill, Sarah (61) resided with her children and husband William Churchill (150, 156). She is buried with her husband in the North Cemetery in West Hartford, Connecticut. The Churchill headstone lists her as; Sarah Sedgwick / His Wife / 1818 – 1910.

Churchill, William (64) was a married farmer, who lived with his family. He was head of household (150, 156). William is buried in the North Cemetery in West Hartford, Connecticut with his wife, the Churchill stone lists him as; William Churchill / 1816 – 1881.

Clark, Alice E. (23) resided with her son and husband, Levi G. Clark (80, 87).

Clark, Edward W. (3) lived with his parents Levi G. and Alice E. (80, 87).

Clark, James M. (18) was single and worked as a farm laborer in the household of John Webster (159, 167).

Clark, Levi G. (40) was a married painter and head of household (80, 87).

Clark, Mary A. (59) was a widow who resided with her son-in-law and daughter, Frank L. and Ruth E. Joyner (138, 144).

Clary, Edward (19) was born in Ireland, single, and worked as a laborer in the household of Michael McDermott (107, 114).

Closson, Jeremiah (62) was single, and worked as a laborer. He was head of household (103, 110) and was also noted as deaf and dumb on the census record.

Cochran, William (29) was born in Ireland, single and worked as a laborer in the household of Thomas Dennis (104, 111).

Coffee, James (25) was born in Ireland, single, and worked as a laborer in the household of William H. Dennis (105, 112).

Connorton, Kate (18) was born in California, single, and worked as a servant in the household of John H. Fish (13, 16). She would appear to be related to Mary Connorton.

Connorton, Mary (16) was born in California, single, and worked as a servant in the household of Jacob Dix (12, 15). She would appear to be related of Kate Connorton.

Cooney, Ella (14) was born in Massachusetts and worked as a servant in the household of David L. Robbins (124, 131).

Cooney, Ephraim (17) was born in New Hampshire and worked as a laborer in the household of R. Wells Kellogg (56, 62).

Cooney, Kate (46) was a widow, born in Ireland, who worked as a domestic servant in the household of Henry M. Robbins (63, 69).

Cooper, Ellen (36) was born in Ireland and resided with her children and husband, John Cooper (55, 61).

Cooper, James (18) was born in Scotland and resided with his sister and parents, John and Ellen (55, 61). He worked as farm laborer.

Cooper, John (41) was born in Scotland, married, and worked as a laborer. He was head of household (55, 61).

Cooper, Katie E. (4) lived with her brother and parents, John and Ellen (55, 61).

Corbin, Aholiab J. (58) was a married a farmer and head of household (141, 147). The tax levy for A.J. Corbin was valued at $3,764 and included the following: 1 house, 68 acres of land, 8 head of livestock, and 1 coach. He is buried in the Newington Cemetery and his headstone reads; Aholiab J. Corbin / 1823 – 1900.

Corbin, Elizabeth (55) was single and resided with her brother, Aholiab J. Corbin (141, 147). She appears to be buried in the Old Stafford Street Cemetery in Stafford, Connecticut. The headstone there reads; Elizabeth Corbin / Died / at Newington, CT / Jan. 10, 1893 / Aged 67.

Corbin, Ellen A. (27) resided with her son, and husband, Frank H. Corbin, in the household of her father-in-law, Aholiab J. Corbin (141, 147).

Corbin, Frank H. (28) was a farmer who lived with his family in the household of her father, Aholiab J. Corbin (141, 147). A tax levy for F.H. Corbin was valued at $100 for 1 piano. Frank was elected as a Town Selectmen at the 4-Oct-1880 town meeting. He also served as a State Republican delegate (see the entry dated 4-Aug-1880 in the Newington happenings section).

Corbin, Harriet (57) resided with family members, and her husband, Aholiab J. Corbin (141, 147). There is a Harriet S. Corbin who died in New Britain, Connecticut on 28-Nov-1905 aged 86-0-8. This is likely the same person, however; the age on the burial permit doesn't coincide with the age given on the census record.

Corbin, Jedidiah D. (2) lived with his parents, Frank H. & Ellen A., in the household of his grandfather, Aholiab J. Corbin (141, 147).

Corr, Barney (55) was born in Ireland, married, and worked as a farm laborer. He was also head of household (127, 134). The census record indicates that he could neither read nor write. The tax levy for Mr. Corr was valued at $231 (surcharge) which included the following: 1 house, 4 acres of land, and 3 head of livestock.

Corr, Bridget (35) was born in Ireland and resided with her children and husband, Barney Corr (127, 134).

Corr, Bridgett (45), was born in Ireland, single, and worked as a servant in the household of Walter F. Brown (69, 76). The census notes her as not being able to read or write.

Corr, Carrie (6) lived with her brother and parents, Barney and Bridget (127, 134).

Corr, John (9) lived with his sister and parents, Barney and Bridget (127, 134).

Costen, Henry (19) was a single black man from North Carolina. He worked as a laborer in the household of R. Wells Kellogg (56, 62).

Cowles, Charles W. (21) was single and worked as a farm laborer in the household of Robert B. Dart (37, 43).

Cowles, Emma H. (22) was born in Virginia and resided with her sister-in-law, children, and husband Geo. E. Cowles (41, 47).

Cowles, Geo. E (28) worked as a machinist and was head of household (41, 47). There is a George E. Cowles buried in the Spring Grove Cemetery in Hartford, Connecticut, the headstone there lists him as; Husband / George E. Cowles / 1852 – 1889.

Cowles, Georgiana (10) attended school that year and lived with the family of her brother, Geo. E. Cowles, and his family (41, 47).

Cowles, Henrietta (10 months) was born in July 1879 and lived with her parents, Geo. E. and Emma H. (41, 47).

Cowles, James B. (23) was single and worked as a farmer in the household of Henry B. Fowler (40, 46). There is a James B. Cowles buried in the Oak Hill Cemetery in Southington, Connecticut, the headstone reads; James B. Cowles / 1859 – 1924. This could potentially be the same person.

Cowles, Sarah J. (6) lived with the family of her brother, Geo. E. Cowles, and his family (41, 47).

Cowles, William J. (3) lived with his parents, Geo. E. and Emma H. (41, 47). The Hale Collection lists a William J. Cowles 1877 – 1903, son, as being buried in the Spring Grove Cemetery in Hartford, Connecticut.

Crocker, Chas. E. (47) was married and worked as a painter. He was head of household (47, 53). Charles Eben Crocker is buried in the Yantic Cemetery in Norwich, Connecticut, the headstone reads; Charles E. / Crocker / 1834 – 1909.

Crocker, Cordelia (13) attended school that year and lived with her siblings and parents, Chas. E. and Olive A. (47, 53).

Crocker, Eben C. (10) lived with his siblings and parents, Chas. E. and Olive A. (47, 53).

Crocker, Edwin W. (16) was in school that year and lived with his siblings and parents, Chas. E. and Olive A. (47, 53). Edwin is buried with other family members in the Yantic Cemetery in Norwich, Connecticut his headstone reads; Edwin W. / Crocker / 1863 – 1915.

Crocker, Howard (5) lived with his siblings and parents, Chas. E. and Olive A. (47, 53).

Crocker, May L. (3) lived with her siblings and parents, Chas. E. and Olive A. (47, 53). May Louise (Crocker) Vinning is buried in Lakewood, Washington at Mountain View Memorial Park. Her headstone there reads; May L. Vining / 1878 – 1961.

Crocker, Olive A. (36) resided with her children and husband, Chas. E. Crocker (47, 53). She is buried in the Yantic Cemetery in Norwich, Connecticut with other family members. Her headstone reads; Olive A. / Crocker / 1842 – 1922.

Crocker, Olive A. (11) attended school that year and lived with her siblings and parents, Chas. E. and Olive A. (47, 53). She is buried in the Fairview Cemetery in West Hartford, Connecticut with her husband, O. Vincent Marsh. The headstone reads; His Wife / Olive S.T. Crocker / 1869 – 1928.

Cunningham, Annie (32) was born in Ireland and resided with her children and husband, Michael Cunningham (116, 123).

Cunningham, John (30) was born in Sweden, single and worked as a farm laborer in the household of Erastus Hart (3, 4).

Cunningham, Mary (8 months) was born in October 1879 and lived with her parents, Michael and Annie (116, 123).

Cunningham, Michael (46) was born in Ireland, worked as a farm laborer, and was head of household (116, 123).

Cunningham, Michael Jr. (4) lived with his parents, Michael and Annie (116, 123).

Cunningham, Theo (28) was single and worked as a farm laborer in the household of Erastus Hart (3, 4).

Cunningham, Thomas (7) was born in New York and lived with his siblings and parents, Michael and Annie (116, 123).

Danaher, Daniel (25) was born in Ireland, single, and worked as a farm laborer in the household of Henry Luce (167, 175). The census record indicates that he could neither read nor write.

Dart, Bertha M. (4) lived with her siblings and parents, Robert B. and Kate (37, 43).

Dart, Fredk. R. (8) lived with his siblings and parents, Robert B. and Kate (37, 43). There is a Fred R. Dart buried in the North Cemetery in Tolland, Connecticut, with his wife, his stone lists dates as 1872 – 1951. This would appear to be a good match for this individual.

Dart, Gertrude A. (6) lived with her siblings and parents, Robert B. and Kate (37, 43).

Dart, Hanford W. (8 months) was born in October 1879. He lived with his siblings and parents, Robert B. and Kate (37, 43). He is buried in the Fairview Cemetery in New Britain, Connecticut, with his wife, the headstone reads; Hanford W. Dart / 1879 – 1963.

Dart, Kate (35) was born in New York and resided with her children and husband, Robert B. Dart (37, 43). Catherine Dart died in Hartford, Connecticut on 14-Aug-1928 at the age of 85-2-27. The Hale Collection notes she is buried in the Newington Cemetery with her husband, Robert and is listed as; Katherine Viele wife of Robert B. 1843 – 1928.

Dart, Norman H. (2) lived with his siblings and parents, Robert B. and Kate (37, 43).

Dart, Robert B. (35) worked as a farmer and was head of household (37, 43). The tax levy for Robert was valued at $110 (surcharge) and was for 4 head of livestock. The burial permit for Robert Bruce Dart states he died in Hartford, Connecticut on 30-Jan-1922 at the age of 76-7-8. The Hale Collection lists him in the Newington Cemetery as; Robert B. Dart 1846 – 1923 with a Civil War marker. There is a disagreement between the burial permit and headstone as to the year of his death.

Davis, Cornelia L. (27) was single and resided with her brother and parents, Willis P. and Mary F. (71, 78). Cornelia Lucretia Davis was baptized in Newington on 18-Jun-1854.

Davis, George D. (18) was single and worked as a farm laborer. He resided in the household of, Willis P. and Mary F. Davis (71, 78). George Dayton Davis, son of George and Mary A., was baptized on 3-Jul-1862 in Newington and later died there on 30-Mar-1926 at the age of 64-8-22. George is buried in the Newington Cemetery with his wife Florence. The Davis stone reads; George D. Davis / 1861 – 1926. The baptism record lists different parents than what the census indicates for George. The census appears to be in error.

Davis, Mary F. (58) resided with her children and husband, Willis P. Davis (71, 78). Mary Tucker married Willis P. Davis, in Newington, on 6-Oct-1840. She is buried in the Newington Cemetery with her husband, the headstone shows her as; Mary Tucker / His Wife / 1822 – 1899.

Davis, Willis P. (64) was a married farmer and head of household (71, 78). His tax levy was valued at $1,558 after an abatement of $3,900 for debt. The items listed were: 3 houses, 102 acres of land, and 33 head of livestock. The property was noted as: Home Lot – 24 ac, Bradley – 15 ac, Welles – 30 ac, Kilbourne – 19 ac, Camp – 8 ac, Wood – 3 ac, and Griswold – 3 ac. Willis married Mary Tucker in Newington on 6-Oct-1840. He is buried with his wife in the Newington Cemetery and is listed as; Willis P. Davis / 1816 – 1891.

Day, Abbie L. (53) was born in New Jersey and resided with her son and husband, Edward T. Day (21, 27). She is buried in the Old North Cemetery in Hartford, Connecticut with her husband Edward. The headstone lists her as; Abbie L. Woodruff / His Wife / 1824 – 1899.

Day, Chas. W. (29) was single, worked as a bookbinder and resided with his parents, Edward T. and Abbie L. (21, 27). He is buried in the Old North Cemetery in Hartford, Connecticut. the headstone there lists him as; Charles W. Day / 1851 – 1931.

Day, Edward T. (63) was married and worked as a bookbinder. He was head of household (21, 27). His tax levy was valued $1,045 (surcharge) and included: 1 house and 1 clock/watch. Edward is buried with his wife in the Old North Cemetery in Hartford, Connecticut, the headstone shows him as; Edward T. Day / 1817 – 1899.

Dee, William Mrs. [Harriet Smart] (75) was noted as a widow and head of household (182, 190). Harriet Smart married William Dee on 8-May-1844 in Newington.

Deming, Ann M. (59) was a widow, who lived with her grand-daughters. She was head of household (164, 172). Ann is buried in the Church Street Cemetery in Newington the headstone there reads: Ann Maria / wife of / Elizur Deming / died Aug. 9, 1886 / aged 65.

Deming, Erastus (20) was single and worked as a farm laborer in the household of Joel Steele (157, 165).

Deming, Frances (54) resided with her children and husband, Selden Deming (165, 173). She died on 31-Mar-1919 aged 93-4-25. Her burial permit indicates she is buried in the Church Street Cemetery in Newington.

Deming, Hattie F. (23) was single and resided with her brother and parents, Selden and Frances (165, 173).

Deming, Jane (35) was single and resided with her grandmother, Ann M. Deming (164, 172).

Deming, Jedediah (60) was widowed, worked as a farmer and lived alone in household (156, 164). His tax levy was valued at $8,109 (surcharge) which included: 3 houses, 90 acres of land, 12 head of livestock, 2 coaches, 1 piano and money at interest of $2,000. The property was listed as: Home Lot – 55 ac, West Side – 14 ac, and Kelsey – 21 ac. Jedediah, son of Jedediah and Mary, was baptized in Newington on 19-Aug-1821. He was appointed as a Juror by the Town Selectmen at the 5-Jan-1880 town meeting. Jedediah Deming Jr. married Nancy A. Whaples on 18-Nov-1846 in Newington and is buried there in the Newington Cemetery with his wife and daughter. The headstone reads; Jedediah Deming / died June 26, 1899 / AE 79.

Deming, Selden (73) was a married farmer and head of household (165, 173). His tax levy was valued at $5,564 which included: 1 house, 140 ½ acres of land, and 7 head of livestock. The property was noted as: Home Lot – 43 ac, Brook – 18 ac, West of Highway – 52 ac, West – 24 ac, and Rimmon – 3 ½ ac. Selden was elected as an Auditor at the town meeting of 4-Oct-1880. He is buried in the Church Street Cemetery in Newington, the stone reads; Selden Deming / Died / July 18, 1885 / Aged 78.

Deming, Thomas A. (33) was single, worked as a farmer and resided with his parents, Selden and Frances (165, 173).

Dennis Families (104, 111) & (105, 112) Both Thomas and William were involved in the manufacturing of bricks in Newington. Some older town maps indicate a brick manufacturing business in the southeast part of town. The many laborers that worked for the Dennis family also lived with them as boarders. Thomas and William Dennis were likely related.

Dennis, Eliza (49) was born in England and resided with her husband, Thomas Dennis (104, 111).

Dennis, Eliza (5) lived with her siblings and parents, William H. and Mary (105, 112).

Dennis, Elizabeth (1) lived with her siblings and parents, Thomas and Eliza (104, 111).

Dennis, Fanny (2) lived with her siblings and parents, William H. and Mary (105, 112).

Dennis, Hannah E. (15) was born in New York and lived with her siblings and parents, Thomas and Eliza (104, 111).

Dennis, James (27) was born in New York, single, and worked as a brick manufacturer with his father. He resided with his siblings and parents, Thomas and Eliza (104, 111).

Dennis, James (3 months) was born in March 1880 and lived with his siblings and parents, William H. and Mary (105, 112).

Dennis, John E. (9) was born in New York, and lived with his siblings and parents, Thomas and Eliza (104, 111).

Dennis, Joseph (13) was born in New York and attended school that year. He lived with his siblings and parents, Thomas and Eliza (104, 111).

Dennis, Mary (23) was born in Ireland and resided with her children and husband, William H. Dennis (105, 112).

Dennis, Thomas G. (3) lived with his siblings and parents, William H. and Mary (105, 112).

Dennis, Thomas (59) was born in England and worked as a brick manufacturer. He was married and also head of household (104, 111). His tax levy was valued at $3,626. Listed items included: 1 house, 19 acres of land, 7 head of livestock, and a $2,000 investment in a manufacturing operation. The investment was likely in his brick manufacturing plant.

Dennis, Thomas (20) was single, born in New York and worked as a laborer in the household of his father, Thomas Dennis (104, 111). He was likely working in the brick manufacturing business with his family.

Dennis, William H. (29) was born in New York and worked as a brick manufacturer. He was head of household (105, 112).

Dix, Alice (3) lived with her siblings and parents, Jacob and Jane (12, 15).

Dix, Charles H. (20) was single and worked as a clerk in a store. He resided with his siblings and parents, Jacob and Jane (12, 15). Charles is buried in the Cedar Hill Cemetery in Hartford, Connecticut with his parents. The Dix stone lists him as; Charles H. Dix / Apr. 30, 1860 – Oct 22, 1918.

Dix, Dwight R. (15) attended school that year and lived with his siblings and parents, Jacob and Jane (12, 15). He is buried in the Cedar Hill Cemetery in Hartford, Connecticut the stone reads; Dwight R. Dix / 1865 – 1915.

Dix, Jacob (49) worked as a tobacco dealer. He was married and head of household (12, 15). His tax levy was valued at $9,206 which included the following: 2 houses, 132 acres of land, 21 head of livestock, 1 coach, 1 clock, 1 piano, and $1,000 cash on hand. The property was listed as follows: Home Lot – 106 ac, Goodrich – 24 ac, and Rimmon – 2 ac. Jacob was appointed as a Juror by the Town Selectmen at the 5-Jan-1880 town meeting and later served as moderator for the town meeting and elections held on 4-Oct-1880. He is buried in the Cedar Hill Cemetery in Hartford, Connecticut with other family members. The headstone lists him as; Jacob Dix / Dec. 18, 1830 / May 18, 1905.

Dix, Jane (45) resided with her children and husband, Jacob Dix (12, 15). She is also buried in the Cedar Hill Cemetery in Hartford, Connecticut with her husband. The headstone shows her as; Jane E. / wife of Jacob Dix / May 10, 1835 / June 1, 1883.

Dix, Jennie L. (10) lived with her siblings and parents, Jacob and Jane (12, 15).

Doherwent this surname also appears to be noted as **Doherwend** in some records.

Doherwent, Charles (45) was born in Germany, worked as a joiner, and was married. He was head of household (148, 154). His tax levy was assessed at $1,185 and included: 1 house, 31 acres of land, and 5 head of livestock. The property was listed as: Home Lot – 11 ac and Rimmon – 20 ac. The Rimmon piece was transferred from the John Webster list to Charles by the Board of Relief.

Doherwent, Chas. F. (5) lived with his siblings and parents, Charles and Elizabeth (148, 154).

Doherwent, Elizabeth (37) resided with her children and husband, Charles Doherwent (148, 154).

Doherwent, Frank H. (9) lived with his siblings and parents, Charles and Elizabeth (148, 154).

Doherwent, Mary A. (8) lived with her siblings and parents, Charles and Elizabeth (148, 154).

Donovan, Catherine (3) lived with her siblings and parents, John and Johanna (162, 170).

Donovan, James (1) lived with his siblings and parents, John and Johanna (162, 170).

Donovan, Johanna (38) was born in Ireland and resided with her children and husband, John Donovan (162, 170). The census record notes that she could neither read nor write.

Donovan, John (40) was born in Ireland, married and worked as a farmer. He was head of household (162, 170). His tax levy was valued at $765 and included: 1 house, 22 acres of land, and 4 head of livestock. The census record indicates that he could not read or write.

Donovan, John (9) lived with his siblings and parents, John and Johanna (162, 170).

Donovan, Lizzie (5) lived with her siblings and parents, John and Johanna (162, 170).

Donovan, Mary A. (7) lived with her siblings and parents, John and Johanna (162, 170).

Donovan, Michael (10) attended school that year and lived with his siblings and parents, John and Johanna (162, 170).

Donovan, Nellie (11) attended school that year and lived with her siblings and parents, John and Johanna (162, 170).

Dorcy, Kate (30) was born in Ireland and resided with her children and husband, William Dorcy (85, 92).

Dorcy, Kate (2) lived with her siblings and parents, William and Kate (85, 92).

Dorcy, Maggie L. (5) lived with her siblings and parents, William and Kate (85, 92).

Dorcy, William (38) was born in Ireland, married, and worked as laborer. He was head of household (85, 92).

Dorcy, William (4) lived with his siblings and parents, William and Kate (85, 92).

Dorman, Abbie R. (44) resided with her children and husband, Walter B. Dorman (137, 143). Abigail Whaples Rockwell, daughter of Robert and Harriet, was baptized in Newington on 10-Aug-1834 and later married Walter B. Dorman there on 25-Oct-1865. She is buried with her husband in the Newington Cemetery and is listed on the Dorman headstone as; Abbie Rockwell / his wife / 1832 – 1914.

Dorman, Hattie R. (10) attended school that year and lived with her siblings and parents, Walter B. and Abbie R. (137, 143). Harriet R. Luce is buried in the Newington Cemetery with her husband, Charles Luce (166, 174). One side of the stone reads; Harriet R. Luce / daughter of / Walter B. and Abbie R. / Dorman. The reverse side; Harriet R. / wife of / Chas. L. Luce / 1869 – 1895.

Dorman, Louis W. (12) attended school that year and lived with his siblings and parents, Walter B. and Abbie R. (137, 143). Lewis W. Dorman is buried with his wife in the Fairview Cemetery in New Britain, Connecticut the headstone reads; Lewis W. Dorman / 1868 – 1954.

Dorman, Robt. W. (13) attended school that year and lived with his siblings and parents, Walter B. and Abbie R. (137, 143). Robert W. Dorman died in West Haven, Connecticut on 15-Jul-1940 at the age of 73-7-17. He is buried in the Newington Cemetery with his parents and wife, the Dorman headstone shows him as; 1867 Robert W. 1940.

Dorman, Walter B. (43) was a married farmer and head of household (137, 143). He married Abigail Rockwell on 25-Oct-1865 in Newington. His tax levy was valued at $1,663 which included: 1 house, 35 acres of land, and 6 head of livestock. The property was listed as: Home Lot – 18 ac, Hopkins – 11 ac, and Churchill – 6 ac. Walter was elected as a Justice of the Peace at the 8-Nov-1880 town meeting. Walter Brewer Dorman died in New Britain, Connecticut on 13-Feb-1922 aged 83-8-19 and is buried with his wife in the Newington Cemetery. The Dorman headstone lists him as; W.B. Dorman / 1838 – 1922.

Dorrity, Annie (20) was born in Ireland, single and worked as a servant in the household of Lemuel W. Camp (117, 124).

Dowd, Charles (10) was in school that year and lived with his siblings and parents, John W. and Margaret (109, 116).

Dowd, Henry (8) lived with his siblings and parents, John W. and Margaret (109, 116).

Dowd, John C. (80) was widowed and resided with his son, John W. Dowd and his family (109, 116).

Dowd, John W. (34) was a married laborer and head of household (109, 116).

Dowd, Maggie (1) lived with her siblings and parents, John W. and Margaret (109, 116).

Dowd, Margaret (37) was born in Ireland and resided with her children and husband, John W. Dowd (109, 116).

Dowd, Rose E. (4) lived with her siblings and parents, John W. and Margaret (109, 116).

Dowd, Seth (79) was widowed and worked as a railroad clerk. He resided with the family of his son-in-law, Edward S. Goodale (98, 105). His tax levy was valued at $1,040 which included: 2 houses, 4 acres of land, and 1 head of livestock. Seth was appointed as a Juror by the Town Selectmen at the 5-Jan-1880 town meeting. He is listed on a Goodale monument in the Newington Cemetery as; Col. Seth Doud / Died Sept. 3, 1885 / Aged 84 Years.

Dower, James (45) was born in Ireland and head of household (25, 31). There is no occupation listed on the census for him. His tax levy was assessed at $456 (surcharge) which included: 1 house, 2 acres of land, and 4 head of livestock. The Hale Collection notes a James Dower 1843 – 1911 buried with his wife Mary in the Mount Saint Benedict Cemetery in Bloomfield, Connecticut. This may be the same person.

Dower, James (11) attended school that year and lived with his siblings and parents, James and Mary (25, 31). The Hale Collection notes a James P. Dower, died 3-Feb-1900 age 33, buried with his wife Delia in the Mount Saint Benedict Cemetery in Bloomfield, Connecticut. This may be the same person.

Dower, John (4) lived with his siblings and parents, James and Mary (25, 31).

Dower, Mary (35) was born in Ireland and resided with her children and husband, James Dower (25, 31). The Hale Collection lists Mary French Dower, wife of James 1847 – 1910 as being buried in the Mount Saint Benedict Cemetery in Bloomfield, Connecticut. This could possibly be the same person.

Dower, Robert (1) lived with his siblings and parents, James and Mary (25, 31).

Dower, William (8) lived with his siblings and parents, James and Mary (25, 31).

Driscol, David (20) was born in Ireland, single, and worked as a farm laborer in the household of Joshua Belden (70, 77).

Dunham, Emerson L. (13) attended school that year and lived with his parents, Lewis W. and Patience L. (59, 65). Emerson is buried in the Centerbrook Cemetery in Essex, Connecticut with his wife. The headstone reads; Dunham / Emerson L. / 1867 – 1962.

Dunham, Lewis W. (36) was a married farmer and head of household (59, 65). Lewis is buried in the Oak Hill Cemetery in Southington, Connecticut. His headstone reads; Lewis W. Dunham / Co. C 6 INF. / Conn Vols / Died Mar. 7, 1908 / AE 65.

Dunham, Patience L. (34) resided with her son and husband, Lewis W. Dunham (59, 65). She is buried in the Oak Hill Cemetery in Southington, Connecticut. Her stone reads; Patience L. / wife of / Lewis W. Dunham / Died Apr. 18, 1922 / AE 76 / Perpetual Care.

Durand, Albert V. (22) was a student, born in New York and married. He resided with his wife, Anna and his siblings in the household of his father, Louis V. Durand (8, 11).

Durand, Allie (10) was born in New York and lived with her grand-father, Louis V. Durand (8, 11). The census record is unclear as to the identity of her parents.

Durand, Anna (25) was born in West Virginia, and resided with her husband Albert V., in the household of her father-in-law, Louis V. Durand (8, 11).

Durand, Elizabeth W. (55) was born in Scotland and resided with her children and husband, Louis V. Durand (8, 11).

Durand, Frances V. (25) was born in New York, single and worked as a music teacher. She resided with her siblings and parents, Louis V. and Elizabeth W. (8, 11).

Durand, Jennie V. (24) was born in New York, single and worked as a landscape artist. She resided with her siblings and parents, Louis V. and Elizabeth W. (8, 11). There was a tax levy for Jennie N. Durand, which may be the same person, it was valued at $2,552 (surcharge) which included: 1 house and 2 acres of land.

Durand, Josephine (2) lived with her grand-parents, Louis V. and Elizabeth W. (8, 11). The census record is unclear as to her parents. It seems likely that her parents were Albert V. and Anna Durand.

Durand, Louis V. (55) was born in Washington D.C. and worked as a physician. He was head of household (8, 11). His tax levy was valued at $220 (surcharge) which included: 1 head of livestock, 1 coach, and 1 piano.

Durand, Louis V. (25) was born in New York, single and a student. He resided with his siblings and parents, Louis V. and Elizabeth W. (8, 11).

Edgecomb, D.W. (39) was married and worked as an insurance adjustor. He was head of household (10, 13). There was a tax levy valued at $1,850, in the name of Daniel W. Edgecomb which included: 1 house and ½ acre of land.

Edgecomb, Kate A. (39) resided with her husband, D.W. Edgecomb (10, 13).

Elliot, John D. (51) was a married clergyman and head of household (60, 66).

Elliot, Mary A. (38) resided with her son and husband, John D. Elliot (60, 66).

Elliot, Thompson C. (17) attended school that year and lived his parents, John D. and Mary A. (60, 66).

Evans, Florence A. (18) was single and resided in the household of Henry Fields (151, 159). It would appear from the record that her mother was probably, Mary A. Evans, sister-in-law of Henry Fields.

Evans, Mary A. (41) was single and resided in the household of her brother-in-law, Henry Fields (151, 159). It would appear that she had a daughter, Florence A. Evans, living with her as well. However, the record does not clearly state this. There also existed a tax levy for Mary valued at $2,029 that included: 60 acres of land, 5 head of livestock and 1 piano. The original levy had 80 acres of land listed but a 20 acre parcel was removed. I believe the 20 ac parcel in question was transferred to her brother-in-law Henry Fields. The remaining property was noted as: Churchill – 27 ac and Patterson – 33 ac. Mary A. Richards, of Wethersfield, Connecticut married Henry D. Evans, of Avon, Connecticut on 21-Aug-1861 in Newington. Her burial permit indicates she died in Colorado Springs, Colorado on 6-Dec-1919 aged 81-3-17. Mary is buried in the Newington cemetery and her headstone reads; Mary A. Richards / wife of / Henry D. Evans / Died Dec. 6, 1919 / Aged 81.

Fairbrothers, Hillyar (22) was a single farm laborer from Vermont who worked in the household of Lester Luce (166, 174).

Fields, Abbie F. (31) resided with family members and her husband, Henry Fields (151, 159). It is likely that she is the sister of Mary A. (Richards) Evans who lived in the same household. Abbie Richards Fields died in New Britain, Connecticut on 4-Feb-1932 aged 83-6-24. She is buried in the Newington Cemetery with her husband Henry the stone reads; His Wife / Abbie Richards / 1848 – 1932.

Fields, Henry (34) was a married farmer and head of household (151, 159). His tax levy was shown as $2,150 which included: 1 house, 29 acres of land, and 2 head of livestock. The property was noted as: Home Lot – 20 ac and East Side 9 – ac. He died in New Britain, Connecticut on 10-Apr-1932 at the age of 86-0-17 and is buried in the Newington cemetery with his wife Abbie the stone shows him as; Henry Fields / 1846 – 1932.

Finnegan, Edwd. W. (14) was in school that year and lived with his siblings and parents, Thomas and Margaret (24, 30). He is buried with other Finnegan family members in the Saint Mary's (old cemetery on Lasalle Street) in New Britain, Connecticut. He is listed on the Finnegan family stone as; Edward W. Finnegan / Jan. 20, 1946.

Finnegan, Hubert (12) attended school and lived with his siblings and parents, Thomas and Margaret (24, 30). He is buried in the Mount Saint Benedict Cemetery in Bloomfield, Connecticut with his wife and daughter. His stone reads; Hubert Finnegan / 1868 – 1941.

Finnegan, John H. (15) worked as a laborer, attended school, and lived with his siblings and parents, Thomas and Margaret (24, 30). He is buried with other Finnegan family members in the Saint Mary's (old cemetery on Lasalle Street) in New Britain, Connecticut. He is listed on the Finnegan family stone as; John H. Finnegan / June 28, 1886.

Finnegan, M. Thomas (17) worked as a laborer, was in school, and lived with his siblings and parents, Thomas and Margaret (24, 30). He is buried with other Finnegan family members in the Saint Mary's (old cemetery on Lasalle Street) in New Britain, Connecticut. He is shown on the Finnegan family stone as; Michael T. Finnegan / Apr. 3, 1886.

Finnegan, Maggie N. (3) lived with her siblings and parents, Thomas and Margaret (24, 30). There is a Margaret F. Van Overstraeten listed on the Finnegan family stone in the Saint Mary's (old cemetery on Lasalle Street) in New Britain, Connecticut. She is shown as; Margaret F. Van Overstraeten / May 11, 1955. This is likely the same person.

Finnegan, Margaret (40) was born in Ireland and resided with her children and husband, Thomas (24, 30). According to the census she could not read or write. She is buried with other family members in the Saint Mary's (old cemetery on Lasalle Street) in New Britain, Connecticut. Margaret is listed on the Finnegan family stone as; his wife / Margaret Curtin / Apr. 18, 1911.

Finnegan, Robert J. (6) lived with his siblings and parents, Thomas and Margaret (24, 30). He is buried with other Finnegan family members in the Saint Mary's (old cemetery on Lasalle Street) in New Britain, Connecticut. He is listed on the Finnegan stone as; Robert J. Finnegan / Dec. 6, 1950.

Finnegan, Thomas (40) was a married farmer and head of household (24, 30). His tax levy was valued at $599 (surcharge) which included: 1 house, 5 acres of land, and 4 head of livestock. He is buried with other family members in the Saint Mary's (old cemetery on Lasalle Street) in New Britain, Connecticut. He is listed on the Finnegan family stone as; Thomas Finnegan / Nov. 3, 1890.

Fish, Adelaide C. (33) resided with her children and husband, John H. Fish (13, 16). The Hale Collection shows her burial in the Fairview Cemetery, West Hartford, Connecticut. She is listed as; Adelaid Braman Fish, wife of John H. 1846 – 1914.

Fish, Alfred B. (7) lived with his siblings and parents, John H. and Adelaide C. (13, 16).

Fish, Daniel W. (26) was a clerk in a store (probably the grocery store of his brother, John H. Fish) and married. He lived in the same dwelling as his brother and was head of his own household (13, 17). Daniel Webster Fish died in Newington on 28-Nov-1930 at the age of 75-5-8. He is buried with his wife and son in the Newington Cemetery and is shown on the Fish family stone as; Daniel W. Fish / 1854 – 1930.

Fish, John H. (30) was married, worked as a grocer, and was head of household (13, 16). His tax levy was valued at $2,050 which included: 1 house and 4 head of livestock. At the town meeting of 4-Oct-1880 he was elected as Scaler of Weights and Measures. John seems to have died in 1936 and is buried in the Fairview Cemetery in West Hartford, Connecticut. The Hale Collection lists him as buried there as well, the headstone shows him as; John H. Fish 1850 – . There is no inscribed death date so it's possible he may be buried elsewhere.

Fish, Martha E. (29) resided with her son and husband, Daniel W. Fish (13, 17). She is buried in the Newington Cemetery. The Fish family stone lists her as; Martha E. Davis / his wife / 1850 – 1921. There is a burial permit for Marilla E. Fish who died in Newington on 15-Apr-1921 aged 70-6-27 that would appear to be the same person.

Fish, Nellie E. (4) lived with her siblings and parents, John H. and Adelaide C. (13, 16). Nellie Emeline Francis died on 31-Jan-1948 aged 71-9-28. Her husband was Thomas A. Francis (53, 59). Nellie is buried in the Newington Cemetery and her headstone reads; Nellie E. Fish / Wife Of / Thomas A. Francis / Apr. 3, 1876 – Jan. 31, 1948.

Fish, Walter J. (1) lived with his parents, John H. and Adelaide C. (13, 16). Walter John Fish died in 1964 and is buried in the Fairview Cemetery in West Hartford, Connecticut near his parents.

Fish, Willis S. (11 months) was born in July 1879 and lived with his parents, Daniel W. and Martha E. (13, 17). Willis died in Newington on 22-Mar-1903 at the age of 23-8-15. He is buried with his parents in the Newington Cemetery the Fish family stone lists him as; Willis S. Fish / 1879 – 1903.

Fitzgerald, James (23) was born in Ireland, single and worked as a farm laborer in the household of Heman Whittlesey (81, 88).

Flarity, John (17) attended school, worked as a farm laborer and lived with his siblings and mother, Mary (100, 107).

Flarity, Kate (12) was in school, worked as a domestic servant and lived with her siblings and mother, Mary (100, 107).

Flarity, Mary (21) was single and worked as a servant. She lived alone in household (96, 103).

Flarity, Mary (45) was a widow born in Ireland and was head of household (100, 107). The census indicates that she could neither read nor write. There existed a tax levy for a Mary and Maurice Flarherty. The spelling difference is somewhat common with this last name. Since she was a widow it's certainly possible that this levy is for her and her deceased husband. It was valued at $616 (surcharge) which included: 1 house, 6 acres of land, and 1 head of livestock.

Flarity, Nellie (13) attended school, worked as a domestic servant, and lived with her siblings and mother, Mary (100, 107).

Ford, Patrick (35) was single, born in Ireland and worked as a laborer in the household of Thomas Dennis (104, 111). The census also noted that he could not read or write.

Forest, Isaac (30) was born in Canada, single and worked as a laborer in the household of Thomas Dennis (104, 111).

Fowler, Henry B. (46) was a married farmer and head of household (40, 46). His tax levy was valued at $27 (surcharge) for 1 head of livestock. He is listed on a headstone in the Salisbury Cemetery in Salisbury, Connecticut with his wife Lucinda, the headstone lists him as; 1834 Henry B. Fowler. There is no inscribed death date so he may be buried elsewhere.

Fowler, Lucinda (44) was born in New York and resided with her daughter and husband, Henry B. Fowler (40, 46). She is buried in the Salisbury Cemetery in Salisbury, Connecticut. The Fowler stone reads; his wife / 1838 Lucinda Dunbar 1914.

Fowler, Mary W. (15) was in school and lived with her parents, Henry B. and Lucinda (40, 46).

Francis, Adeline H. (46) resided with her children, mother and husband, Pratt Francis (52, 58). Adeline Hurd Francis died in Newington on 22-Mar-1930 aged 96-2-11 and is buried in the Newington Cemetery with her husband. The Francis headstone lists her as; Adeline Hurd / his wife / Jan. 11, 1834 – Mar. 22, 1930.

Francis, Arlan (22) was single and worked as a farmer. He resided with his siblings and parents, Pratt and Adeline H. (52, 58). Arlan P. Francis died in Westmoreland, New Hampshire on 25-Oct-1935 at the age of 77-4-28. He is buried in the Newington Cemetery with his parents and wife, the Francis headstone lists him as; Arlan Pratt Francis / May 30, 1858 – Oct. 26, 1935. There is a 1 day discrepancy between the death date on the burial permit and inscribed headstone.

Francis, Augusta L. (40) resided with her daughter and husband, Robert Francis (15, 20). She is buried next to her husband Robert in the Fairview Cemetery in New Britain, Connecticut. Her stone reads; L. Augusta Francis / 1834 – 1925.

Francis, Caroline S. (40) resided with her children and husband, Joseph J. Francis (18, 24). Caroline Spencer Francis died in Newington on 7-Apr-1923 aged 82-11-2 and is buried in the Newington Cemetery. Her headstone reads; Caroline S. Francis / Died / April 7, 1923 / Aged 83 Yrs.

Francis, Chas. S. (3) lived with his siblings and mother, Ellen D. Francis (53, 59). Charles S. Francis died in Danielson, Connecticut on 22-Aug-1941 at the age of 64-7-9 and is buried in the Newington Cemetery. His headstone reads as follows; Charles S. Francis / Jan. 13, 1877 – Aug. 22, 1941 / Q.M. SERG. Co. H, 3 REG'T / Conn. Vol. Infantry / Spanish American War.

Francis, Ellen D. (40) was noted as married, but there is no husband shown in the household. She was head of household (53, 59). A tax levy for the Chas. S. Francis heirs (he died in 1877) was shown as $3,728 and included: 1 house, 80 acres of land, and 12 head of livestock. The property was listed as follows: House Lot – 2 ac, Wells – 5 ac, Brook – 2 ac, North Corner – 24 ac, Whaples – 7 ac, Andrus – 8 ac, West – 8 ac, Brush Hill – 4 ac, Pear Swamp – 3 ac, New Britain Road – 14 ac and Railroad Pasture – 3 ac. Ellen Boyington, of Wethersfield, Connecticut married Charles S. Francis, also of Wethersfield, in Newington on 18-Jun-1863. Ellen E. Francis died in Newington on 08-Aug-1925 aged 85-6-17 and is buried with her husband in the Newington Cemetery. The Francis headstone shows her as; His Wife / Ellen E. Boyington/ Jan. 22, 1840 – Aug. 8, 1925.

Francis, Emma L. (6) lived with her siblings and parents, Joseph J. and Caroline S. (18, 24).

Francis, Fredk. W. (16) was in school that year and lived with his siblings and parents, Pratt and Adeline H. (52, 58).

Francis, Geo. B. (22) was an apprentice to a machinist, single and resided with his siblings and parents, Joseph J. and Caroline S. (18, 24).

Francis, George (42) was married, worked as a laborer, and head of household (120, 127). The Hale Collection shows him buried in the Hamden Plains Cemetery in Hamden, Connecticut with his wife Mary. He is listed as; George B. Francis Nov. 11, 1839 – Apr 25, 1914.

Francis, Hannah (76) was a widow who resided with her son George Francis (120, 127). The Hale Collection shows at least two possible burials that could be a match for Hannah, one in Norwich, Connecticut and another in New Haven, Connecticut. Further research is needed to clarify.

Francis, Herbert C. (15) was in school and lived with his siblings and mother, Ellen D. (53, 59). He died in Newington on 22-May-1919 at the age of 53-10-15. Herbert is buried in the Newington Cemetery with his parents, the Francis headstone shows him as; Herbert C. their son / July 7, 1865 – May 22, 1919.

Francis, Howard W. (15) attended school and lived with his siblings and parents, Joseph J. and Caroline S. (18, 24). Howard died in Warwick, Rhode Island on 15-Jun-1947 aged 81-2-14. He is buried in the Newington Cemetery and shares a headstone with his wife, the stone lists him as; Francis / Howard / 1865 – 1947.

Francis, Jessie A. (10) was in school and lived with her parents, Robert and Augusta L. (15, 20).

Francis, Joseph J. (57) was born in Massachusetts, married, and worked as the RR Depot Master. He was head of household (18, 24). Joseph is buried in the Newington Cemetery the headstone reads; Joseph J. Francis / Died / June 29, 1891 / Aged 82 yrs.

Francis, Lena B. (4) lived with her siblings and parents, Joseph J. and Caroline S. (18, 24). She is buried in the Newington Cemetery with her husband, Charles R. Osborn (77, 84). The Osborn family headstone shows her as; Lena B. Francis, His Wife / Nov. 28, 1876 – Oct. 18, 1962.

Francis, Martha A. (19) was single and worked as a telegraph operator. She resided with her siblings and parents, Joseph J. and Caroline S. (18, 24).

Francis, Mary (30) was born in New York and resided with her mother-in-law and husband, George Francis (120, 127). The Hale Collection shows her burial in the Hamden Plains Cemetery in Hamden, Connecticut with her husband George. She is listed as; Mary A. Loper wife Nov. 29, 1849 – Dec. 13, 1925.

Francis, Pratt (49) was a married farmer and head of household (52, 58). His tax levy was shown as $5,550 which included: 1 house, 77 acres of land, 19 head of livestock, $1,800 in Insurance stock and money at interest of $200. The property was identified as: House Lot – 12 ac, West – 8 ac, Stone Hill – 30 ac, Brush Hill – 3 ac, River – 5 ac, Pear Swamp – 3 ac, and Railroad – 16 ac. At the 4-Oct-1880 town meeting Pratt was elected to serve on the Board of Relief. He is buried in the Newington Cemetery with his wife. The Francis family stone lists him as; Pratt Francis / Sept. 22, 1831 – Nov. 18, 1910.

Francis, Robert (43) was a married machinist and head of household (15, 20). His tax levy was valued at $2,545 after $200 was abated. Items on the list included: 2 houses, 1 head of livestock, 1 coach, and 1 piano. He was appointed as a Juror by the Town Selectmen at the 5-Jan-1880 town meeting and later elected to serve on the Board of Relief at the 4-Oct-1880 meeting. Robert appears to be buried next to his wife Augusta in the Fairview Cemetery in New Britain, Connecticut. His stone reads; Robert Francis / 1835 – 1914.

Francis, Thos. A. (11) was in school and lived with his siblings and mother, Ellen D. Francis (53, 59). Thomas Arthur Francis died in Newington on 11-Jun-1945 at the age of 77-0-5 and is buried in the Newington Cemetery. The stone reads; Thomas A. Francis / June 6, 1868 – June 11, 1945 / A Faithful Servant.

Francis, Valina A. (46) was single and resided with her brother-in-law, John Webster (159, 167). She had a tax levy valued at $540 for 18 acres of land.

French, Ann (27) was born in Scotland and resided with her children and husband, John French (112, 119). The census notes that she could neither read nor write at this time.

French, John H. (2 months) born in April 1880. He lived with his siblings and parents, John and Ann (112, 119).

French, John (29) was born in Ireland, married, and worked as a laborer. He was head of household (112, 119). The census indicated that he could neither read nor write. His tax levy was valued at $255 and included: 1 house, 3 ½ acres of land, and 2 head of livestock.

French, Mary (3) lived with her siblings and parents, John and Ann (112, 119).

French, Thomas P. (7) lived with his siblings and parents, John and Ann (112, 119).

French, William (5) lived with his siblings and parents, John and Ann (112, 119).

Fricke, Joseph (27) was married, born in Germany and worked as a laborer in the household of Thomas Dennis (104, 111). His wife was not listed with him on the census.

Gaffney, Mary (42) was married, born in Ireland and worked as a servant in the household of James B. Griswold (175, 183).

Gaines, J.C. (35) was a married machinist and head of household (5, 7). The house his family resided in was shared with the Marcy family.

Gaines, Kate C. (31) resided with her son and husband, J.C. Gaines (5, 7).

Gaines, Robt. A. (4) lived with his parents, J.C. and Kate C. (5, 7).

Gaylord, Jos. C. (54) was a single farmer who lived alone in household (4, 5). Joseph Camp Gaylord, son of Edwin and Lucy, was baptized on 2-Oct-1825 in Newington. His tax levy was shown as $1,360 after an abatement of $152. The items listed were: 1 house and 38 acres of land. He is buried in the Newington Cemetery and his headstone reads; Joseph C. Gaylord / Died / Aug. 26, 1895 / Aged 70 yrs.

Gibbons, Flora A. (23) was born in Massachusetts, single and worked as a housekeeper in the household of her cousin Hudson H. Stoddard (46, 52). She is also the likely related to Stella P. Gibbons who was working in the same household.

Gibbons, Stella P. (18) was born in Massachusetts, single and worked as a servant in the household of her cousin, Hudson H. Stoddard (46, 52). It is likely she is related to Flora A. Gibbons.

Giden, Christopher (28) was born in Ireland and worked as a laborer in the household of Thomas Dennis (104, 111).

Gilbert, Ella (8) lived with her siblings and parents, Louis and Josephine (125, 132).

Gilbert, Flora (2) lived with her siblings and parents, Louis and Josephine (125, 132).

Gilbert, Howard (3) lived with his siblings and parents, Louis and Josephine (125, 132).

Gilbert, Josephine (38) resided with her children and husband, Louis Gilbert (125, 132).

Gilbert, Louis (50) was married, worked as a house painter, and head of household (125, 132).

Gilbert, Maria A. (73) was a widow who resided in the household of her son-in-law, Saml. H. Kilbourne, (62, 68). She is buried in the Newington Cemetery and her headstone reads; Maria A. Wife Of / Ira Gilbert / 1805 – 1888.

Gladding, Emily J. (35) was born in Indiana and resided with her husband, James H. Gladding (118, 125). She is buried in the Fairview Cemetery in New Britain, Connecticut, next to her husband. The headstone reads; Emily J. Gladding / Born Nov. 17, 1846 / Died Jan. 19, 1910.

Gladding, James H. (56) was a married farmer and head of household (118, 125). His tax levy was valued at $425 which included: 1 house and 1 head of livestock. James is buried in the Fairview Cemetery in New Britain, Connecticut, next to his wife. His headstone reads; James H. Gladding / 1st Light Battery / Conn. Vols. / Born Feb. 13, 1824 / Died Apr. 2, 1896 / Sleep Soldier Sleep / Thy Labor Is Done / Sweet Be Thy Rest / Thy Victory Is Won.

Gladding, Wilbur (24) was a single farm laborer who worked in the household of Ellen D. Francis (53, 59). There is a Wilbur Gladding, who died in 1943, that is buried in the West Cemetery in Plainville, Connecticut, this could be the same person.

Goodale, Benjamin (9) lived with his siblings and parents, Edward S. and Emma R. (98, 105). He is buried in the Newington Cemetery with his wife, the headstone reads; Benjamin H. Goodale / 1871 – 1970.

Goodale, Edward C. (12) was in school and lived with his siblings and parents Edward S. and Emma R. (98, 105). He is buried in the Newington Cemetery with his wife Bertha, the Goodale stone shows him as; Goodale / Edward S. / 1868 – 1954.

Goodale, Edward S. (36) was married, worked as a tinner, and was head of household (98, 105). His tax levy was valued at $55 (surcharge) for 2 head of livestock. Edward Selden Goodale died in Newington on 19-Jan-1933 aged 88-11-24. He is buried with his wife in the Newington Cemetery, the Goodale headstone reads; Edward S. Goodale / Died Jan. 19, 1933 / Aged / 88 Years.

Goodale, Emma R. (35) was born in Kentucky and resided with her children and husband, Edward S. Goodale (98, 105). She died in Newington on 28-Jul-1928 aged 82-10-13 and is buried in the Newington Cemetery with her husband. The Goodale headstone shows her as; Emma R. Goodale / Died / July 28, 1928 / Aged / 82 Years.

Goodale, Henry (3) lived with his siblings and parents, Edward S. and Emma R. (98, 105).

Goodrich, Louis Mrs. [Violetia (Case) Goodrich] (70) was noted as married and worked as a servant in the household of Chas. K. Atwood (50, 56). Lewis Goodrich died in May 1880 and is buried in the Newington Cemetery. It would appear she should have been noted as a widow rather than married on the census record. A tax levy existed for Mrs. Lewis Goodrich which was valued at $220 (surcharge) for a house. Lewis Goodrich, of Wethersfield, Connecticut married Violetia Case, of Simsbury, Connecticut in Newington on 29-Apr-1827. In the Little Rock Township Cemetery of Plano, Illinois there is a Mrs. Violetia Goodrich who died in 1893 that is buried there. This burial would appear to be Mrs. Goodrich.

Gregory, Thos. (34) was single, born in England and worked as a laborer in the household of Thomas Dennis (104, 111). The census record indicates that he could not read or write.

Griswold, Alice M. (8) lived with her siblings and parents, Chester B. and Mary A. (66, 73).

Griswold, Chester B. (45) was married, worked as a carpenter and was head of household (66, 73). His tax levy was valued at $407 which included: 1 house and 3 head of livestock. He died in Newington on 24-April-1902 at the age of 67-6-16. Chester is buried in the Newington Cemetery next to his wife, his headstone reads; Chester B. Griswold / Oct. 8, 1834 / Apr. 24, 1902.

Griswold, Ellen A. (33) resided with her daughter and husband, James B. Griswold (175, 183). She is buried in the Cedar Hill Cemetery in Hartford, Connecticut. The Griswold family stone lists her as; 1847 Ellen A. His Wife 1935.

Griswold, James B. (34) was a married farmer and head of household (175, 183). He is buried in the Cedar Hill Cemetery in Hartford, Connecticut. The Griswold family headstone shows him as; 1845 James B. Griswold 1918.

Griswold, Mary A. (37) resided with her children and husband, Chester B. Griswold (66, 73). Mary is buried next to her husband in the Newington Cemetery. Her headstone reads; Mary A. / Wife Of / Chester B. Griswold / Aug. 29, 1839 / June 4, 1896 / At Rest.

Griswold, Mary S. (13) was in school and lived with her siblings and parents, Chester B. and Mary A. (66, 73).

Griswold, Nancy (78) was a widow who resided with the family of her son, Chester B. Griswold (66, 73). Nancy Blinn, of Wethersfield, Connecticut married Chester Griswold on 11-Dec-1828 in Newington. She is buried in the Newington Cemetery and her headstone reads; Nancy / Wife Of / Chester Griswold / Died July, 31, 1891 / AE 90.

Griswold, Nellie G. (8) lived with her parents, James B. and Ellen A. (175, 183). She is buried in the Cedar Hill Cemetery in Hartford, Connecticut with her family and husband, Anson A. Mills. The Griswold family headstone shows her as; 1871 Nellie G. His Wife 1950.

Griswold, Nellie (7) lived with her siblings and parents, Chester B. and Mary A. (66, 73).

Hart, Emma (30) resided with her husband, Erastus Hart (3, 4). She was noted as suffering from consumption at the time of the census. Emma is buried in the Fairview Cemetery in New Britain, Connecticut. Her stone reads; Emma J. Messenger / Wife Of / Erastus S. Hart / 1850 – 1917.

Hart, Erastus (30) was a married farmer and head of household (3, 4). His tax levy was shown as $525 for 21 head of livestock. He is buried with his wife in the Fairview Cemetery in New Britain, Connecticut, his stone reads; Erastus S. Hart / 1849 – 1933.

Hawley, Emily C. (61) was single and resided with her brother, Samuel C. Hawley (90, 97). Emily is buried with her brother in the North Cemetery in West Hartford, Connecticut. The stone lists her as; Emily G. Hawley / Died July 12, 1896 / Aged 77.

Hawley, Samuel C. (60) was a single farmer and head of household (90, 97). His tax levy was valued at $1,275 which included: 1 house, 23 acres of land, and 2 head of livestock. He is buried with his sister, Emily, in the North Cemetery in West Hartford, Connecticut. The headstone shows him as; Samuel C. Hawley / Died Jan. 15, 1900 / Aged 80.

Healy, Maggie M. (41) was listed as single, but may have been a widow. She resided with her brother William Boardman (34, 40).

Hills, Abram (81) was widowed and lived alone in household (181, 189). Abram was also listed on the Supplemental Schedule for the 1880 census. He was shown in the pauper section with the disability of "old age". He may have died after the census, see order 57 in the Selectmen report.

Holcomb, Sarah F. (79) was a widow who resided with the family of her son-in-law, Joseph Camp (43, 49).

Holland, Arthur (25) was born in England, single and worked as a farm laborer in the household of Aholiab J. Corbin (141, 147).

Hopkins, Timothy (35) was born in Ireland, single and worked as a laborer in the household of William H. Dennis (105, 112).

House, Agnes G. (2) lived with her siblings and parents, Franklin W.E. and Elba A. (125, 131). She is buried in the Lakeview Cemetery in Bridgeport, Connecticut and shares the headstone with a younger brother, Willie. The House headstone reads; Agnes G. / Died Dec. 2, 1885 / Aged 8 Years / Children Of / Frank W.E. & Elba M. / House.

House, Elba A. (32) resided with her children and husband, Franklin W.E. House (125, 131). She is buried in the Lakeview Cemetery in Bridgeport, Connecticut, and is listed on The House headstone with two other women (sisters perhaps?) the stone reads; Elba House / 1848 – 1942.

House, Eva L. (5) lived with her siblings and parents, Franklin W.E. and Elba A. (125, 131).

House, Franklin W.E. (35) worked as a painter, was married, and head of household (125, 131). His tax levy was valued at $1,015 which included: 1 house, 2 acres of land, and 2 head of livestock.

House, Howard F. (5) lived with his siblings and parents, Franklin W.E. and Elba A. (125, 131).

House, Olive A. (9) lived with her siblings and parents, Franklin W.E. and Elba A. (125, 131).

Hoye, Annie (2) lived with her siblings and parents, Charles and Mary (35, 41).

Hoye, Charles (40) was married, born in Ireland, and worked as a laborer. He was head of household (35, 41).

Hoye, Ellen (7) was born in New York and lived with her siblings and parents, Charles and Mary (35, 41).

Hoye, Francis (13) was in school and lived with his siblings and parents, Patrick E. and Mary E. (14, 18). The Hale Collection notes a Francis P. Hoye 1867 – 1913 buried in the Mount Saint Benedict Cemetery in Bloomfield, Connecticut. This could be the same individual.

Hoye, John J. (17) attended school, worked as a laborer, and lived with his siblings and parents, Patrick E. and Mary E. (14, 18).

Hoye, Kate E. (40) was born in Ireland and resided with her children and husband, Peter Hoye (14, 19).

Hoye, Kate (20) was born in New York, worked as a domestic servant, and resided with her siblings and parents, Charles and Mary (35, 41).

Hoye, Lizzie (8) lived with her siblings and parents, Peter and Kate E. (14, 19).

Hoye, Lizzie (16) was born in Ireland and worked as a servant in the household of Marcus L. Stoddard (20, 26).

Hoye, Margaret E. (10) was in school and lived with her siblings and parents, Patrick E. and Mary E. (14, 18).

Hoye, Mary E. (40) was born in Ireland and resided with her children and husband, Patrick E. Hoye (14, 18).

Hoye, Mary K. (15) was in school and lived with her siblings and parents, Patrick E. and Mary E. (14, 18).

Hoye, Mary K. (5) lived with her siblings and parents, Peter and Kate (14, 19).

Hoye, Mary (33) was born in Ireland and resided with her children and husband, Charles Hoye (35, 41).

Hoye, Michael (5) lived with his siblings and parents, Charles and Mary (35, 41).

Hoye, Patrick E. (48) was born in Ireland, married, and worked as a laborer. He was head of household (14, 18). His tax levy was valued at $645 which included: 1 house and 5 head of livestock.

Hoye, Patrick (1) was born in Sept. 1879. He lived with his siblings and parents, Charles and Mary (35, 41).

Hoye, Peter E. (5) lived with his siblings and parents, Patrick E. and Mary E. (14, 18).

Hoye, Peter (32) was born in Ireland, worked as a laborer and was head of household (14, 19).

Hoye, Rosie A. (12) was in school and lived with her siblings and parents, Patrick E. and Mary E. (14, 18).

Hoye, Thos. H. (4) lived with his siblings and parents, Peter and Kate E. (14, 19).

Hubbard, Eliza (68) was a widow, worked as a nurse and resided with her son-in-law, Horace Whaples (65, 72).

Hubbard, Margaret (60) was born in Massachusetts and resided with family members and her husband, William Hubbard (76, 83). Margaret B. Hubbard died in Newington on 23-Jun-1905, aged 85-8-15 and is buried in the Newington Cemetery. The Hubbard stone reads; Margaret B. Topliff / Wife Of / William Hubbard / Died / June 23, 1905 / Aged 85.

Hubbard, William A. (33) was single, worked as a farm laborer and resided with his parents, William and Margaret (76, 83). He was baptized William Albert Hubbard on 10-Oct-1847 in Newington and is buried there in the Newington Cemetery. His headstone reads; William Albert / Hubbard / Died May 6, 1914 / Aged 67 Yrs. / Donor Of The / Margaret B. Hubbard Fund.

Hubbard, William (68) was a married farmer and head of household (76, 83). The tax levy for Wm. Hubbard was valued at $3,306 which included the following: 2 houses, 67 ¼ acres of land, 11 head of livestock, and money at interest of $100. The property was listed as: Home Lot – 4 ac, Wells – 14 ac, Mountain – 15 ac, Hurlbut – 21 ac, Swamp – 4 ¾ ac, Fitch – 4 ½ ac, and Black Oak – 4 ac. He is buried in the Newington Cemetery. The Hubbard stone reads; William Hubbard / Died / July 15, 1888 / Aged 76.

Hunn, Anna L. (30) was born in New York and resided with her son and husband, Lucius E. Hunn (51, 57).

Hunn, Edwin L. (2 ½) lived with his parents, Lucius E. and Anna L. (51, 57).

Hunn, Lucius E. (50) was married, worked as a government clerk and was head of household (51, 57).

Hunn, Minerva C. (69) was a widow and head of household (6, 8). Minerva C. Rogers married Albert S. Hunn on 2-Dec-1840 in Newington. A tax levy existed for the Albert S. Hunn Estate that was valued at $6,765 which included: 4 houses, 89 ½ acres of land, and money at interest of $1,000. The property was identified as: Home Lot – 14 ac, West – 58 ac, Clark – 15 ac and, Howe – 2 ½ ac. She is buried with her husband in the Newington Cemetery, the Hunn headstone lists her as; Minerva C. Hart / His Wife / Died Oct. 21, 1887 / Aged 76 Yrs. 7 Mos.

Hurd, Signora C. (70) was listed as married on the census but her husband wasn't enumerated with her. She resided in the household of her son-in-law, Pratt Francis (52, 58).

Irwin, Katie (8) lived with her siblings and parents, Richard and Mary L. (123, 130).

Irwin, Mary L. (33) was born in Ireland and resided with her children and husband, Richard Irwin (123, 130).

Irwin, Mary R. (4) lived with her siblings and parents, Richard and Mary L. (123, 130).

Irwin, Richard H. (1) lived with his siblings and parents, Richard and Mary L. (123, 130).

Irwin, Richard (44) was born in Ireland and married. He worked as a farmer and was head of household (123, 130).

Irwin, Robert W. (6) lived with his siblings and parents, Richard and Mary L. (123, 130).

Johnson, Peor (25) was single, born in Sweden and worked as a farm laborer in the household of Joshua Belden (70, 77).

Jordan, Moses (18) was single, worked as a farm laborer and lived alone in household (82, 89).

Jordan, William (17) was a single farm laborer who worked in the household of Lyman Wetherell (89, 96).

Joseph, Edward (29) was single, born in Sweden, and worked as a farm laborer in the household of Walter F. Brown (69, 76).

Joyner, Frank L. (28) was born in Massachusetts. He was a married farmer who was head of household (138, 144).

Joyner, Robert O. (70) was married and born in Massachusetts. He worked as a farmer and was head of household (84, 91). His tax levy was valued at $1,783 which included: 1 house, 48 acres of land, and 6 head of livestock. Robert, of Egremont, Massachusetts, married, Sarah C. Wells, in Newington on 26-Oct-1842. He is buried in the Newington Cemetery, the headstone reads; Robert O. Joyner / Apr. 28, 1810 / Oct. 26, 1893.

Joyner, Robert W. (34) was born in Massachusetts and single. He worked as a farmer and resided with his parents, Robert O. and Sarah C. (84, 91). Robert is buried in the Cedar Hill Cemetery in Hartford, Connecticut with his wife, Lucy B. Kappell (93, 100). The Joyner headstone reads; Robert Wells Joyner / 1845 – 1919 / Co. G 20 Regt. / Conn. Vols.

Joyner, Ruth E. (18) was married and resided with her husband, Frank L. Joyner (138, 144). Her headstone in the Windsorville Cemetery in Hartford, Connecticut reads; Ruth E. Clark / Wife Of / Frank L. Joyner / Aug. 21, 1861 / Aug. 3, 1901.

Joyner, Sarah C. (61) was married and resided with her son and husband, Robert O. Joyner (84, 91). Sarah C. Wells, married Robert O. Joyner, of Egremont, Massachusetts, in Newington on 26-Oct-1842. She is buried in the Newington Cemetery and her headstone reads; Sarah C. Wells / Wife Of / Robert O. Joyner / Aug. 9, 1819 / Dec. 29, 1909.

Kapp, Hettie (76) was a widow born in Germany. She resided in the household of her son-in-law, Jacob Bader (136, 142).

Kappell, Fanny E. (68) was listed as married but there is no husband in the household only two daughters. She was head of household (93, 100). It appears her husband, George W. Kappell, died in 1876. There was a tax levy for Mrs. Geo. W. Kappell that was valued at $1,670 which included: 1 house, 16 acres of land, 5 head of livestock, and $500 of bank stock. Fanny is buried in the Cedar Hill Cemetery in Hartford, Connecticut with her husband and some children. The headstone reads; Fanny S. Kappell / 1811 – 1890.

Kappell, Fanny S. (32) was single and resided with her sister and mother, Fanny E. Kappell (93, 100). She is buried in the Cedar Hill Cemetery in Hartford, Connecticut with her parents. The headstone shows her as; Fanny S. Kappell / 1847 – 1899.

Kappell, Lucy B. (30) was single and resided with her sister and mother, Fanny E. Kappell (93, 100). She is buried with her husband, Robert W. Joyner (84, 91), in the Cedar Hill Cemetery in Hartford, Connecticut. The Joyner headstone reads; Lucy Bunce Kappell / His Wife / 1850 – 1936.

Keefe, Patrick (30) was born in Ireland, single and worked as a laborer in the household of Thomas Dennis (104, 111).

Kellogg, Henry L. (64) was a married farmer and head of household (44, 50). Henry Laurens Kellogg, son of Martin Jr. and Mary, was baptized on 5-May-1816 in Newington. His second marriage to, Laura K. Camp, of Wethersfield, Connecticut took place on 6-Feb-1866 in Newington. His tax levy was valued at $6,120 which included: 5 houses, 74 acres of land, 13 head of livestock, 2 coaches, and 1 clock. The property was listed as: Home Farm – 38 ac and South – 36 ac. There is also a levy for the Martin Kellogg Estate [Martin was his father, also see the entry dated 23-Mar-1880 in the Newington Happenings section] that was valued at $4,085 which included: 1 house, 122 acres of land, and 13 head of livestock. Henry was elected as an Assessor at the 4-Oct-1880 town meeting. He is buried in the Newington Cemetery with both of his wives. The Kellogg monument shows him as; Henry L. Kellogg / Died June 3, 1895 Aged 79 Yrs.

Kellogg, Henry L. Jr. (21) was single and resided with his father and step-mother, Henry L. and Laura C. (44, 50). Henry Laurens Kellogg, son of Henry L. and Julia A., was baptized in Newington, on 6-Aug-1859 and later died in Hartford, Connecticut on 15-Mar-1919 at the age of 60-2-1. He is buried with his parents in the Newington Cemetery. The Kellogg monument lists him as; Henry Laurens Son Of / H.L. & J.A. Kellogg / June 14, 1859 – Mar. 15, 1919.

Kellogg, Julia (23) was single and resided in the home of her uncle, R. Wells Kellogg (56, 62).

Kellogg, Laura C. (48) resided with her step-son and husband, Henry L. Kellogg (44, 50). Laura K. Camp, of Wethersfield, Connecticut married Henry L. Kellogg on 6-Feb-1866 in Newington and died there on 24-May-1904 at the age of 72-3-17. She is buried in the Newington Cemetery with her husband. The Kellogg headstone lists her as; Laura K. Camp Wife Of H.L. Kellogg / Died May 24, 1904 Aged 72 Yrs.

Kellogg, R. Wells (66) was a single farmer and head of household (56, 62). His tax levy was shown as $18,317 which included: 1 house, 257 acres of land, 32 head of livestock, 1 coach, $3,167 in bank stock, $500 in insurance stock, money at interest of $3,500, and $951 cash on hand. The property was identified as: Home Lot – 81 ac, Kellogg – 8 ac, West – 64 ac, Williams – 15 ac, Hurlbut – 20 ac, Whittlesey – 31 ac, Wells – 6 ac, J. Corner – 5 ac, 50 acre – 9 ac, and Pond – 18 ac. Roger Welles Kellogg, son of Martin Jr. and Mary, was baptized on 2-Jul-1815 in Newington. He was elected as a Hayward (Town official in charge of fences and enclosures) at the 4-Oct-1880 town meeting. Roger is buried in the Newington Cemetery with other family members, the Kellogg stone shows him as; Roger Welles Kellogg / Born June 12, 1813 / Died Mar. 6, 1881.

Kelly, Hugh (29) was single, born in Ireland and worked as a laborer in the household of Thomas Dennis (104, 111). The census notes him as not being able to read or write.

Kelly, John (30) was single, born in Ireland and worked as a farm laborer in the household of David L. Robbins (124, 131).

Kerwin, Hugh (40) was single and born in Ireland. He worked as a farmer and was head of household (151, 157). His tax levy was valued at $3,414 which included: 1 house, 78 acres of land, and 9 head of livestock. The Hale Collection notes Hugh is buried in the Old St. Mary's Cemetery in New Britain, Connecticut. He is listed as; Hugh Kerwin died Jan. 2, 1919 age 85 y.

Kerwin, John (36) was born in Ireland, single and worked as a farmer. He resided with family members in the household of his brother Hugh Kerwin (151, 157). The Hale Collection notes John is buried in the Old St. Mary's Cemetery in New Britain, Connecticut. He is listed as; John Kerwin died Mar. 19, 1907 age 74 y.

Kerwin, Mary (58) was single and born in Ireland. She resided in the household of her brother, Hugh Kerwin (151, 157). The Hale Collection notes Mary is buried in the Old St. Mary's Cemetery in New Britain, Connecticut. She is listed as; Mary Kerwin died Sep. 29, 1898 age 76 y.

Kerwin, Rose (92) was a widow from Ireland. She resided with her children in the household of her son, Hugh Kerwin (151, 157). The Hale Collection notes Rose is buried in the Old St. Mary's Cemetery in New Britain, Connecticut, and is listed as; Rose Kerwin died Dec. 21, 1883 age 96 y. born in Co. Fermanach Ireland.

Kilbourne, Effie M. (9) was in school and lived with her brother and parents, Saml. H. & Sarah M. (62, 68).

Kilbourne, Elbert E. (35) was a widowed farmer and head of household (73, 80). Elbert Edwards Kilbourne, son of Erastus and Elmina, was baptized in Newington on 29-Jul-1849. His tax levy was shown as $781 (surcharge) which included: 1 house and 12 acres of land. He is buried with his wife, Alice J., in the Newington Cemetery. The Kilbourne stone lists him as; Elbert E. Kilbourne / Died Dec. 18, 1890 / Aged 46 Yrs.

Kilbourne, Erastus (78) was listed as married on the census but his wife Elmina had died in 1877. He was a farmer and head of household (72, 79). His tax levy was valued at $1,245 which included: 1 house, 1 store, 7 acres of land, and 6 head of livestock. Erastus is buried with his wife, in the Newington Cemetery the headstone shows him as; Erastus Kilbourne / Died Aug. 20, 1886 / Aged 85 Yrs.

Kilbourne, Erastus Jr. (49) was single and worked as a grocer probably in his father's store. He resided with his siblings and father, Erastus Kilbourne (72, 79). Erastus Kilbourne, son of Erastus and Elmina, was baptized in Newington on 27-May-1832. He was appointed as a Juror by the Town Selectmen at the 5-Jan-1880 town meeting. His headstone in the Newington Cemetery lists him as; Erastus K. Kilbourne / Died / May 28, 1907 / Aged 76 Yrs.

Kilbourne, Franklin H. (6) lived with his sister and father, Elbert E. Kilbourne (73, 80). He is buried in the Newington Cemetery with his parents and listed on the headstone as; Frank E. Kilbourne / 1874 – 1916.

Kilbourne, Horace (51) was a single farmer who resided with his father, Erastus Kilbourne (72, 79). He had a tax levy valued at $968 (surcharge) which included: 1 house and 7 acres of land. Horace, son of Erastus and Elmina, was baptized in Newington on 16-Mar-1829. He is buried in the Newington

Cemetery with his wife, Elizabeth. The Kilbourne headstone lists him as; Horace Kilbourne / Died / Aug. 18, 1899 / Aged 70 Yrs.

Kilbourne, Mary W. (53) was single and resided with her siblings and father, Erastus Kilbourne (72, 79). Mary Webb Kilbourne, daughter of Erastus and Elmina, was baptized in Newington on 16-Sep-1827. She is buried with other family members in the Newington Cemetery, the Kilbourne stone shows her as; Mary W. Kilbourne / Died / April 12, 1888 / Aged 60 Yrs. / 10 Mos.

Kilbourne, Nancy (42) was single and resided with her siblings and father, Erastus Kilbourne (72, 79). Nancy, daughter of Erastus and Elmina, was baptized in Newington on 9-Sep-1838 and is buried in the Newington Cemetery with other family members. The Kilbourne headstone shows her as; Nancy Kilbourne / Died / Nov. 14, 1905 / Aged 68 Yrs.

Kilbourne, Nellie L. (11) was in school and lived with her brother and father, Elbert E. Kilbourne (73, 80). Nellie died in Hartford, Connecticut on 21-Apr-1929 at the age of 59-10-27 and is buried in the Newington Cemetery with her husband Raphael S. Kilbourne (62, 68). She is shown on the headstone as; Nellie L. His Wife / 1869 – 1929.

Kilbourne, Raphael F. (14) was in school and lived with his sister and parents, Saml. H. and Sarah M. (62, 68). Raphael Samuel Kilbourne died in Hartford, Connecticut on 19-Apr-1932 at the age of 65-11-22 and is buried in the Newington Cemetery with his wife, Nellie L. Kilbourne (73, 80). The headstone lists him as; Raphael S. Kilbourne / 1866 – 1932.

Kilbourne, Saml. H. (40) was married, worked as a carpenter and was head of household (62, 68). His tax levy was listed as $902 (surcharge) which included: 1 house, 9 acres of land, and 1 head of livestock. Samuel was elected as the Pound Keeper at the 4-Oct-1880 town meeting. Samuel Hart Kilbourne, son of Henry and Emeline G., was baptized in Newington on 28-Mar-1841, and died there at the age of 71-8-19, on 30-May-1912. He is buried in the Newington Cemetery with his wives. The Kilbourne headstone shows him as; Samuel H. Kilbourne / 1840 – 1912.

Kilbourne, Sarah M. (37) resided with her children and husband, Saml. H. Kilbourne (62, 68). She died in Wethersfield, Connecticut on 4-Dec-1920 at the age of 77-10-23 and is buried in the Newington Cemetery with her husband. The Kilbourne stone lists her as; Sarah M. His Wife / - 1920. No birth year is shown on the stone.

Kirkham, Frances H. (19) was a single school teacher who resided with her siblings and parents, John S. and Harriet P. (94, 101). Frances Harriet Kirkham was baptized in Newington on 21-Jul-1861.

Kirkham, Harriet P. (53) resided with her children and husband, John S. Kirkham (94, 101). Harriet Prudence Atwood, daughter of Josiah and Prudence, was baptized in Newington on 19-Aug-1827 she married John S. Kirkham there on 1-Dec-1859. Harriet is buried with John in the Newington Cemetery, the headstone lists her as; Harriet Prudence / Wife Of / John S. Kirkham / Died Dec. 1, 1882.

Kirkham, J. Henry (15) was in school and lived with his siblings and parents, John S. and Harriet P. (94, 101). He is buried in the Newington Cemetery with his wife Lillian. The Kirkham stone shows him as; John H. Kirkham / April 18, 1865 - April 13, 1939.

Kirkham, John S. (54) was a married farmer, and head of household (94, 101). John Stoddard Kirkham, son of William and Sofia, was baptized in Newington on 20-Aug-1826 and later married Harriet P. Atwood, of Wethersfield, Connecticut there on 1-Dec-1859. His tax levy was valued at $5,996 after a $500 abatement for debt. Items on the list included: 3 houses, 127 acres of land, 16 head of livestock, and 1 piano. His property was listed as: Home Lot – 30 ac, Back – 59 ac, Hart – 7 ac, River – 19 ac, Elias – 4 ac, Wells – 4 ac, and Sprout – 4 ac. At the town meeting of 4-Oct-1880 John was elected as Town Clerk and Registrar and later as a Justice of the Peace at the 8-Nov-1880 meeting. He died in Newington on 8-Feb-1918 aged 91-10-2 and is buried in the Newington Cemetery. He is listed on the Kirkham headstone as; John S. Kirkham / Apr. 6, 1825 / Feb. 8, 1918.

Kirkham, Mary A. (13) was in school and lived with her siblings and parents, John S. and Harriet P. (94, 101). Mary Atwood Kirkham was baptized in Newington on 1-Nov-1866.

Kirkham, Sophia (84) was a widow and head of household (95, 102). She died shortly after the census and is buried in the Newington Cemetery with her husband William. She is listed on the Kirkham headstone as; Sophia Leffingwell / His Wife / Died / 14-Nov-1880 / Aged 84.

Kirkham, Thomas A. (18) was a single farmer who resided with his siblings and parents, John S. and Harriet P. (94, 101). Thomas Atwood Kirkham was baptized in Newington on 4-Sep-1862 and died in Bridgeport, Connecticut on 4-Nov-1931 at the age of 69-7-27. He is buried with his wife, Fanny, in the Newington Cemetery. The Kirkham stone shows him as; Thomas A. Kirkham / March 7, 1862 / Nov. 4, 1931.

Kofner, Caroline (31) was born in Germany and resided with her children and husband, Frank Kofner (177, 185).

Kofner, Charles (9) lived with his brother and parents, Frank and Caroline (177, 185).

Kofner, Frank (41) was born in Germany, married, and worked as a laborer. He was head of household (177, 185).

Kofner, William (6) lived with his brother and parents, Frank and Caroline (177, 185).

Larson, Martha M. (23) was born in Sweden, single and worked as a servant in the household of Erastus Hart (3, 4).

Lasiter, Redmond (21) was born in North Carolina, single and worked as a farm laborer in the household of Heman Whittlesey (81, 88).

Latimer, Alice M. (7) lived with her siblings and parents, Franklin C. and Mary D. (168, 176). Alice Mary Latimer, daughter of Franklin C. was baptized in July of 1873 in Newington, the record lists no mother or date for the baptism.

Latimer, Anna C. (4) lived with her siblings and parents, Franklin C. and Mary D. (168, 176).

Latimer, Franklin C. (44) was married, worked as a farmer, and was head of household (168, 176). His tax levy was valued as $12,038 which included: 2 houses, 188 acres of land, 24 head of livestock, 2 coaches, 2 clocks, 1 piano, $1,260 in bank stock and money at interest of $2,200. He married his first wife, Mary N. Seymour, in Newington on 5-Dec-1866, she died in 1869.

Latimer, Mary D. (32) was married and resided with her children and husband, Franklin C. Latimer (168, 176). She appears to have been the second wife of Franklin.

Latimer, Maud L. (2) lived with her sisters and parents, Franklin C. and Mary D. (168, 176).

Lea, Timothy (25) was single, born in Ireland and worked as a farm laborer in the household of Jacob Bader (136, 142).

Livingston, Thomas (23) was born in Ireland, single and worked as a farm laborer in the household of William G. Wells (170, 178).

Luce, Charles L. (15) was in school and lived with his parents, Joshua C. and Joanna B. in the household of his grandfather, Lester Luce (166, 174). Charles Lester Luce died in Newington on 3-Jul-1944 at the age of 79-5-6 and is buried in the Newington Cemetery. His headstone reads; Charles L. Luce / 1865 – 1944.

Luce, Flora J. (35) was married and resided with her son and husband, Henry Luce (167, 175). She is buried in the Newington Cemetery with her family. The Luce stone lists her as; Flora J. Francis / 1842 His Wife 1924.

Luce, Harry B. (3) lived with his parents, Henry and Flora J. (167, 175). Harry Burton Luce died in Newington on 21-Apr-1924 at the age of 46-8-3 and is buried in the Newington Cemetery. The Luce family headstone lists him as; Harry B. / 1877 Their Son 1924.

Luce, Henry (62) was a married farmer and head of household (167, 175). His tax levy was for $4,150 which included: 1 house, 47 acres of land, 15 head of livestock, and $1,000 in bank stock. The property was listed as: Webster Lot – 15 ac, Francis – 12 ac, and Stone Hill – 20 ac. He is buried with his family in the Newington Cemetery. The Luce family stone shows him as; Henry Luce / 1818 – 1891.

Luce, Joanna B. (43) was married and resided with her husband, Joshua C. Luce, and her children in the household of her father-in-law, Lester Luce (166, 174). She is incorrectly noted on the census as a daughter of Lester rather than a daughter-in-law. Joanna Brewer Luce died in Newington on 24-Dec-1913 at the age of 76-9-8 and is buried in the Newington Cemetery. The Luce headstone lists her as; Joanna Brewer Luce / 1837 – 1913.

Luce, Joshua C. (54) was a married farmer who resided in the household of his father, Lester Luce (166, 174). Joshua Chauncey Luce, son of Lester and Sofia, was baptized in Newington on 20-Aug-1826. His tax levy was valued at $9,357 which included: 1 house, 221 ½ acres of land, and 37 head of livestock. The property was identified as: Land – 190 ac, Richards – 26 ac, and Green Swamp – 5 ½ ac. Joshua is buried in the Newington Cemetery with his parents and wife. The Luce headstone lists him as; Joshua C. Luce / 1826 – 1884.

Luce, Lester (82) was widowed and head of household (166, 174). He married Sophia Lattimer, of Wethersfield, Connecticut on 25-Nov-1817 in Newington. She died in 1877. He is buried in the Newington Cemetery with his wife. The Luce headstone shows him as Lester Luce / 1797 – 1883.

Luce, Mary L. (20) was single and resided with her siblings and parents, Joshua C. and Joanna B. in the household of her grandfather, Lester Luce (166, 174). Mary L. Carpenter is buried in the West Cemetery in Plainville, Connecticut, with her husband Samuel, the Carpenter headstone lists her as; Mary L. His Wife / Died Apr. 1, 1946 / Aged 86 Yrs.

Luce, Nellie (7) lived with her siblings and parents, Joshua C. and Joanna B. in the household of her grandfather, Lester Luce (166, 174).

Lund, Frank A. (23) was single, born in Sweden and worked as a farm laborer in the household of John Webster (159, 167).

Luther, Lucy A. (57) resided with her daughter and husband, Martin Luther (110, 117). She is buried with her husband in the Fairview Cemetery in New Britain, Connecticut. The Luther headstone shows her as; Lucy / His Wife / 1823 – 1902.

Luther Lucy E. (33) was single and resided with her parents, Martin and Lucy A. (110, 117). She is buried with her parents in the Fairview Cemetery in New Britain, Connecticut. The Luther stone lists her as; Lucy Ella Luther / 1847 – 1917.

Luther, Martin (61) was born in New York, married and worked as a mill builder. He was also head of household (110, 117). His tax levy was shown as $1,281 which included: 1 house, 9 acres of land, 1 mill, and 3 head of livestock. He is buried in the Fairview Cemetery in New Britain, Connecticut with his wife and children. The Luther stone shows him as; Martin Luther / 1819 – 1897.

Lynch, John (25) was born in Ireland, single and worked as a farm laborer in the household of Henry M. Robbins (63, 69).

Lyons, Andrew C. (14) was in school and worked as a farm laborer. He lived with his siblings and parents, Peter W. and Mary (158, 166). The Hale Collection shows him buried with family members in the St. Mary's Cemetery in New Britain, Connecticut as; Andrew Lyons died Nov. 27, 1891 age 25 y. 3 m.

Lyons, Ellen E. (20) resided with her siblings and parents, Peter W. and Mary (158, 166).

Lyons, Maggie (10) was in school and lived with her siblings and parents, Peter W. and Mary (158, 166).

Lyons, Mary (34) was born in Ireland, married and resided with her children and husband, Peter W. Lyons (158, 166). The census indicates that she could not read or write. The Hale Collection lists her in the St. Mary's Cemetery in New Britain, Connecticut as; Mary A. Lyons wife of Peter died July 7, 1900 age 59 y. The age on the census record and Hale differ by 5 years but this appears to be the same person.

Lyons, Peter J. (12) was in school and worked as a farm laborer. He lived with his siblings and parents, Peter W. and Mary (158, 166). The Hale Collection shows him buried with family members in the St. Mary's Cemetery in New Britain, Connecticut as; Peter J. Lyons died Jan. 28, 1895 age 27 y. 5 m.

Lyons, Peter W. (43) was born in Ireland and married. He was a farmer and head of household (158, 166). His tax levy was valued at $723 which included: 1 house, 6 acres of land, and 3 head of livestock. The Hale Collection shows him buried with family members in the St. Mary's Cemetery in New Britain, Connecticut as; Peter Lyons died Dec. 29, 1898 age 65 y.

Lyons, Thomas E. (16) was in school and worked as a farm laborer. He lived with his siblings and parents, Peter W. and Mary (158, 166).

Mackin, Thos. (40) was single, born in Ireland and worked as a farm laborer in the household of, Henry M. Robbins (63, 69).

Mahaney, Daniel (25) was born in Ireland, single and worked as a laborer in the household of William H. Dennis (105, 112).

Mahoney, Darius (35) was born in Ireland and married. He worked as a laborer and was head of household (57, 63).

Mahoney, Mary (33) was born in Ireland and resided with her husband, Darius Mahoney (57, 63).

Marcy, J. Andrew (25) was married, worked as a clerk in a store and was head of household (5, 6).

Marcy, Lizzie (27) resided with her husband, J. Andrew Marcy (5, 6).

Markley, Anna (50) was born in Ireland, married and resided with her children and husband, Thomas Markley (121, 128). Ann is buried in the Saint Mary Cemetery in New Britain, Connecticut with her husband. The Markley headstone lists her as; Ann Wife Of / Thomas Markley / Died Mar. 5, 1885 / Aged 50 Yrs.

Markley, Grace A. (20) was single and resided with her siblings and parents, Thomas and Anna (121, 128). Grace is buried in the Saint Mary Cemetery in New Britain, Connecticut with her husband, Michael Coholan. The headstone reads; His Wife / Grace Ann Markley / Died Apr. 21, 1941 / Aged 81 Yrs. 7 Mos.

Markley, Lizzie M. (27) was single and resided with her siblings and parents, Thomas and Anna (121, 128). She is buried with her parents in the Saint Mary Cemetery in New Britain, Connecticut. The Markley stone lists her as; Lizzie M. Markley / Died Feb. 5, 1885 / Aged 32 Yrs.

Markley, Philip J. (25) was single and studying law. He resided with his siblings and parents; Thomas and Anna (121, 128). Philip is buried in the Saint Mary Cemetery in New Britain, Connecticut with his brother. He is listed on the headstone as; Philip J. Markley / Died / July 25, 1902 / Aged 47 Yrs. 5 Mos.

Markley, Thomas (55) was married and born in Ireland. He worked as a drover and was head of household (121, 128). His tax levy was valued at $3,611 which included the following: 1 house, 58 acres of land, 8 head of livestock, swine, 1 coach, 1 clock and 1 piano. Thomas was elected as a Hayward (Town official in charge of fences and enclosures) at the 4-Oct-1880 town meeting. He is buried with family members in the Saint Mary Cemetery in New Britain, Connecticut. The Markley stone lists him as; Thomas Markley / Died / June 19, 1883 / Aged 63 Yrs. / Native Of Tipperary Ireland.

Markley, William T. (22) was single and worked as a farm laborer. He resided with his siblings and parents, Thomas and Anna (121, 128). William was appointed as a Juror at the town meeting of 5-Jan-1880. He is buried in the Saint Mary Cemetery in New Britain, Connecticut with his brother. The headstone lists him as; William T. Markley / Died July 15, 1886 / Aged 28 Yrs. 11 Mos.

Martin, Elizabeth (13) worked as a servant in the household of Heman Whittlesey (81, 88). Two other Martin children also worked in that household, so it seems they could have been related.

Martin, Elulia (13) was in school and lived with her parents, J.W. and Josephine (174, 182). She is buried in the East Cemetery in Manchester, Connecticut. The headstone reads; Elulia Martin / Alvord / 1867 – 1957.

Martin, Frank (15) worked as a farm laborer in the household of Heman Whittlesey (81, 88). It seems that he could be related to the other two Martin children who worked in that household.

Martin, J.W. (38) was married, worked as a trading salesman and was head of household (174, 182). He is buried in Manchester, Connecticut in the East Cemetery. His headstone reads; Joel W.W. Martin / 1843 – 1912.

Martin, Jane (35) was married, born in Ireland and resided with her children and husband, Thomas Martin (113, 120). The census states that she could neither read nor write.

Martin, Jane (8) lived with her siblings and parents, Thomas and Jane (113, 120).

Martin, Josephine (40) was married and resided with her daughter and husband, J.W. Martin (174, 182). She is buried in the East Cemetery in Manchester, Connecticut. Her stone reads; Josephine Loomis / Martin / 1842 – 1919.

Martin, McCormick (6) lived with his siblings and parents, Thomas and Jane (113, 120).

Martin, Patrick (15) worked as a farm laborer in the household of Heman Whittlesey (81, 88). It seems that he could be related to the other two Martin children who worked in that household.

Martin, Thomas (40) was married, worked as a laborer and was head of household (113, 120). His tax levy was valued at $295. There is an entry next to the total that says "abated for debt" it is unclear if the entire amount was abated. Items on the levy included: 1 house, 2 acres of land, and 2 head of livestock. The census record indicates he could not write.

Martin, Thomas (11) was in school and lived with his siblings and parents, Thomas and Jane (113, 120).

McCarty, John (35) was born in Ireland, single and worked as a laborer in the household of Thomas Dennis (104, 111).

McDermott, Bridgett (22) was married and born in Ireland. She resided with her children and husband, Michael McDermott (107, 114). The census notes her as unable to read or write.

McDermott, John (2) was born in Ireland and lived with his sister and parents, Michael and Bridgett (107, 114).

McDermott, Julia (3) was born in Ireland and lived with her brother and parents, Michael and Bridgett (107, 114).

McDermott, Michael (37) was born in Ireland, single and worked as a laborer in the household of Thomas Dennis (104, 111). The census indicated that he could neither read nor write.

McDermott, Michael (30) was married and born in Ireland. He worked as a laborer and was head of household (107, 114).

McGinnes, Ann (40) was born in Ireland and married. She resided with her children and husband, Patrick McGinnes (54, 60). According to the census she could not read or write.

McGinnes, Margaret (6 mos.) born in Nov. 1879. Lived with her siblings and parents, Patrick and Ann (54, 60).

McGinnes, Patrick (40) was married and born in Ireland. He worked as a laborer and was head of household (54, 60). The census indicated that he could not read or write.

McGinnes, Peter (3) lived with his siblings and parents, Patrick and Ann (54, 60).

McGinnes, Thomas (5) lived with his siblings and parents, Patrick and Ann (54, 60).

McGrath, Ann M. (33) was born in Ireland and resided with her children and husband, John McGrath (150, 158). The Hale Collection notes an Ann McGrath buried with her husband in the Old St. Mary's Cemetery in New Britain, Connecticut. She was shown as the wife of John and died Aug. 18, 1885 age 36 y. This could be the same person.

McGrath, James (1) lived with his siblings and parents, John and Ann M. (150, 158).

McGrath, John (40) was married and born in Ireland. He worked as a farmer and was head of household (150, 158). The Hale Collection notes a John McGrath buried with his wife in the Old St. Mary's Cemetery in New Britain, Connecticut. He was shown as having died Apr. 2, 1890 age 47 y. This could be the same person.

McGrath, John (4) lived with his siblings and parents, John and Ann M. (150, 158).

McGrath, Kate (5) lived with her siblings and parents, John and Ann M. (150, 158).

McGrath, Mary A. (10) lived with her siblings and parents, John and Ann M. (150, 158).

McGrath, Stephen (8) lived with his siblings and parents, John and Ann M. (150, 158).

Merrills, Charles W. (6) lived with his parents, J.O. and Nellie G. (68, 75). The Hale Collection notes a Charles Merrills is buried in the Spring Grove Cemetery in Hartford, Connecticut, there are no dates listed for him. This could be this individual.

Merrills, J.O. (32) was married and worked as a farmer. He was also head of household (68, 75). A tax levy existed for John Merrills for $495 (surcharge) for 1 house.

Merrills, Nellie G. (27) was married and resided with her son and husband, J.O. Merrills (68, 75).

Miller, Charles (29) was single, born in Ireland and worked as a laborer in the household of Thomas Dennis (104, 111). The census notes him as unable to read or write.

Miskell, Catherine (40) was married, born in Ireland. She resided with her son and husband, Michael Miskell (173, 181). The census states she could neither read nor write.

Miskell, John (14) was in school and lived with his parents, Michael and Catherine (173, 181).

Miskell, Kate (17) was in school and worked as a servant in the household of Emily F. Robbins (172, 180). She is likely the daughter of Michael and Catherine Miskell (173, 181).

Miskell, Michael (50) was a married farmer from Ireland who was head of household (173, 181). Michael Miscall had a tax levy valued at $330 (surcharge) which included: 1 house and 4 head of livestock.

Mitchell, Nellie (17) was single and born in Vermont. She worked as a servant in the household of Shubael H. Whaples (6, 9). The census notes she could not read or write.

Monahan, Ann (3) lived with her siblings and parents, James and Mary (163, 171).

Monahan, James (38) was a married farmer from Ireland and head of household (163, 171). The census indicated the he could neither read nor write. His tax levy was valued at $695 which included: 1 house, 18 acres of land, and 5 head of livestock.

Monahan, Katie (5) lived with her siblings and parents, James and Mary (163, 171).

Monahan, Maggie (1) lived with her siblings and parents, James and Mary (163, 171).

Monahan, Mary (35) was married, born in Ireland, and resided with her children and husband, James Monahan (163, 171). She could not read or write.

Monahan, Mary (7) lived with her siblings and parents, James and Mary (163, 171).

Monahan, Michael (9) lived with his siblings and parents, James and Mary (163, 171).

Morgan, Frank G. (16) worked as a farm laborer and lived with his siblings and parents, Gaylord and Mary E. (91, 98). He appears to have died in 1917 and is buried in the West Cemetery in Plainville, Connecticut.

Morgan, Frank (28) was single and worked as a farm laborer in the household of Henry M. Robbins (63, 69).

Morgan, Gaylord (43) was born in New York and married. He worked as a farmer and was head of household (91, 98). His tax levy was $440 (surcharge) for 1 house. He died in Newington on 1-Oct-1903 at the age of 67-2-15 and is buried in the Newington Cemetery. His headstone reads Gaylord Morgan / Co. B 22nd Inf. / Conn. Vols. / Died Oct. 1, 1903 / AE 67.

Morgan, George A. (13) was in school and lived with his siblings and parents, Gaylord and Mary E. (91, 98). He died in Hartford, Connecticut on 13-Sep-1926 at the age of 39-2-23 and is buried in the Newington Cemetery with his family. His stone reads; Father / George A. Morgan / 1866 – 1926.

Morgan, Hattie M. (8) lived with her siblings and parents, Gaylord and Mary E. (91, 98). She is buried in the Newington Cemetery with her husband, Charles L. Backus. The Backus headstone shows her as, His Wife / 1871 Hattie M. Morgan 1953.

Morgan, Henry A. (19) was single, worked as a farm laborer and resided with his siblings and parents, Gaylord and Mary E. (91, 98). He is buried in the Oak Hill Cemetery in Southington, Connecticut with his wife. The Morgan headstone shows him as; Henry A. Morgan / 1861 – 1900.

Morgan, Mary E. (37) was born in Massachusetts and resided with her children and husband, Gaylord Morgan (91, 98). She is buried in the Newington Cemetery and her headstone reads, Mary B. Morgan / Died / Mar. 19, 1924 / Aged 83 Y'rs.

Morgan, Walter L. (10) was in school and lived with his siblings and parents, Gaylord and Mary E. (91, 98). Walter Lewis Morgan died in Kensington, Connecticut on 16-Oct-1949 at the age of 79 and is buried in the Newington Cemetery. His stone reads, Walter L. Morgan / Died / Oct. 16, 1949 / Aged 79 Yrs.

Morris, Francis S. (23) was single and worked as a farmer. He resided with his brother and parents, Samuel W. and Jane H. (101, 108). Francis is listed on the Morris stone in the Wethersfield Village Cemetery, in Wethersfield Connecticut. He is shown as; Frank E. Morris / Born Mar. 23, 1857 / Died May 10, 1883.

Morris, Jane H. (55) resided with her sons and husband, Samuel W. Morris (101, 108). She is buried in the Wethersfield Village Cemetery, in Wethersfield, Connecticut with her husband. The stone shows her as; Jane H. Savage / Widow of Samuel W. Morris / Wife of Charles S. Daniels / Born May 1, 1825 / Died April 30, 1894.

Morris, Samuel W. (54) was a married farmer who was head of household (101, 108). A tax levy existed for the Samuel W. Morris Estate so he died after the census was enumerated. The levy was valued at $2,031 and included: 1 house, 48 acres of land, and 4 head of livestock. He is buried in the Wethersfield Village Cemetery, in Wethersfield, Connecticut with his wife. The headstone lists him as; Samuel W. Morris / Born Nov. 15, 1822 / Died Sept. 8, 1880.

Morris, William S. (22) was single and worked as a farmer. He resided with his brother and parents, Samuel W. and Jane H. (101, 108).

Morton, Samuel (28) was single and worked as a farm laborer in the household of Henry M. Robbins (63, 69).

Mulcahay, Edward (20) was born in Ireland, single and worked as a laborer in the household of William H. Dennis (105, 112).

Mulcahy, Fanny F. (19) was single and worked as a servant in the household of Edward T. Day (21, 27).

Mulcahy, James (44) was married and born in Ireland. He worked as a laborer and was head of household (38, 44). He had a tax levy valued at $55 (surcharge) for 2 head of livestock.

Mulcahy, James (12) lived with his siblings and parents, James and Margaret (38, 44).

Mulcahy, John (10) was in school and lived with his siblings and parents, Thomas and Kate (26, 32).

Mulcahy, Kate (42) was born in Ireland and resided with her children and husband, Thomas Mulcahy (26, 32). The census notes she could not write.

Mulcahy, Maggie (8) lived with her siblings and parents, Thomas and Kate (26, 32).

Mulcahy, Margaret (44) was born in Ireland and resided with her children and husband, James Mulcahy (38, 44). The census indicates she could neither read nor write.

Mulcahy, Margaret (8) lived with her siblings and parents, James and Margaret (38, 44).

Mulcahy, Mary E. (13) was in school and lived with her siblings and parents, Thomas and Kate (26, 32).

Mulcahy, Michael (16) was in school and lived with his siblings and parents, Thomas and Kate (26, 32).

Mulcahy, Michael (18) was single and worked as a laborer. He resided with his siblings and parents, James and Margaret (38, 44). The census notes he could neither read nor write.

Mulcahy, Thomas (45) was married and born in Ireland. He worked as a farmer and was head of household (26, 32). He had a tax levy valued at $456 (surcharge) which included: 1 house, 2 acres of land, and 2 head of livestock. The census indicates that he could not write.

Mulcahy, Thomas (14) was in school and lived with his siblings and parents, Thomas and Kate (26, 32).

Murphy, Neil (28) was born in England, single, and worked as a laborer in the household of William H. Dennis (105, 112). Also see the 5-Jul-1880 entry in the Newington Happenings section.

Murray, Andrew (20) was single, born in New York, and worked as a farm laborer in the household of, Thomas Markley (121, 128).

Muttley, Albert (30) was single, born in Canada, and worked as a laborer in the household of Thomas Dennis (104, 111). He is likely related to Falie Muttley.

Muttley, Falie (35) was single, born in Canada, and worked as a laborer in the household of Thomas Dennis (104, 111). He is likely related to Albert Muttley.

Neilson, Peter (23) was from Sweden and single. He worked as a farm laborer in the household of Shubael H. Whaples (6, 9).

Nelson, John (38) was married and born in Sweden. He worked as a laborer and was head of household (106, 113). The census indicates that he could not read or write. According to an 1899 transcription of the Newington Cemetery there was a John Nelson buried there. The transcription indicated he was born in Sweden with dates listed as 26-Mar-1854 and 12-Apr-1894, this is likely the same person.

Nelson, John Jr. (3) was born in Massachusetts and lived with his parents, John and Margaret (106, 113).

Nelson, Margaret (35) was born in Ireland and resided with her son and husband, John Nelson (106, 113).

Nolan, Catherine (40) was born in Ireland and resided with her daughters and husband, Patrick Nolan (16, 21).

Nolan, Lizzie (3) lived with her sister and parents, Patrick and Catherine (16, 21).

Nolan, Mary (2) lived with her sister and parents, Patrick and Catherine (16, 21).

Nolan, Patrick (40) was born in Ireland and married. He worked as a laborer and was head of household (16, 21). His tax levy was valued at $907 (surcharge) which included: 1 house and 1 head of livestock.

Norman, Matthew (28) was from Ireland, single, and worked as a laborer in the household of William H. Dennis (105, 112).

O'Brien, Dennis (20) was from Ireland, single, and worked as a farm laborer in the household of Franklin C. Latimer (168, 176).

O'Brien, John (25) was born in Ireland, single, and worked as a farm laborer in the household of David L. Robbins (124, 131).

Olmstead, Elizabeth M. (2) was born in Iowa and lived with her parents, Henry J. and Mary S. (17, 23).

Olmstead, Henry J. (32) was married and worked as a merchant. He was head of household (17, 23).

Olmstead, Mary S. (26) resided with her daughter and husband, Henry J. Olmstead (17, 23).

Osborne, Charles R. (7) lived his siblings and parents, Newton and Mary A. (77, 84). He died in Newington on 21 Aug-1921 at the age of 47-10-10 and is buried there in the Newington Cemetery with his wife. The Osborne stone lists him as; Charles R. Osborn / Oct. 2, 1873 - Aug. 11, 1921. There appears to be a discrepancy of the date of death between the burial permit and headstone.

Osborne, Mary A. (31) resided with her children and husband, Newton Osborne (77, 84). Mary A. Osborn died in Newington on 28-Sep-1934 and is buried in the Newington Cemetery with her husband. The Osborn headstone lists her as; Mary A. Clark / His Wife / Aug. 24, 1848 – Sept. 28, 1934.

Osborne, Newell C. (6) lived with his brother and parents, Newton and Mary A. (77, 84).

Osborne, Newton (28) was a married farmer and head of household (77, 84). He was appointed as a Juror by the Town Selectmen at the 5-Jan-1880 town meeting. Newton is buried in the Newington Cemetery with his family. The headstone shows him as; Newton Osborn / June 28, 1851 – Jan. 8, 1927.

Osborne, Shelden (1) lived with his brother and parents, Newton and Mary A. (77, 84).

Phelps family (155, 163). Samuel O. Phelps is listed as the head of household for this family, however; no relationships are listed on the census record for the other people in the household. I have assumed these individuals to be his wife and children since he is noted as married on the census.

Phelps, Adelia (3) lived with her siblings and parents, Samuel O. and Mary (155, 163).

Phelps, Mary (24) resided with her children and husband, Samuel O. Phelps (155, 163).

Phelps, Mary (5) lived with her siblings and parents, Samuel O. and Mary (155, 163).

Phelps, Samuel O. (27) was married, worked as a farmer and was head of household (155, 163). His tax levy was shown as $99 (surcharge) for 3 head of livestock.

Phelps, Samuel (2) lived with his siblings and parents, Samuel O. and Mary (155, 163).

Pimm, Alfred (4) lived with his siblings and parents, Ebenezer and Ann (30, 36).

Pimm, Ann (36) was born in England and married. She resided with her children and husband, Ebenezer Pimm (30, 36). Ann is buried in the Newington Cemetery with her husband Ebenezer. The Pimm headstone shows her as; Ann Bladon / His Wife / 1844 – 1917.

Pimm, Annie (11) was born in England and attended school. She lived with her siblings and parents, Ebenezer and Ann (30, 36).

Pimm, Ebenezer (40) was from England and married. He worked as a carpenter and was head of household (30, 36). His tax levy was valued at $110 (surcharge) for 1 house. Ebenezer E. Pimm died in Newington on 12-Feb-1925 aged 84-10-30 and is buried with family members in the Newington Cemetery. The Pimm stone lists him as; Ebenezer E. Pimm / 1840 – 1925.

Pimm, Effie (9) lived with her siblings and parents, Ebenezer and Ann (30, 36). Effie Frances Pimm died in Hartford, Connecticut on 1-May-1947 at the age of 76-6-11 and is buried in the Newington Cemetery. Her headstone reads; Effie Frances Pimm / Daughter of E.E. and / Ann Bladon Pimm / 1870 – 1947.

Pimm, Lillian (14) was born in England and attended school. She lived with her siblings and parents, Ebenezer and Ann (30, 36).

Pimm, William (8) lived with his siblings and parents, Ebenezer and Ann (30, 36).

Pollard, Lucy (19) was single and worked as a servant in the household of William G. Wells (170, 178).

Post, Elizabeth (56) was a widow who resided with her son. She was head of household (78, 85).

Post, George E. (19) was single and worked as an apprentice to a machinist. He resided with his mother, Elizabeth Post (78, 85).

Potter, Fanny M. (7) lived with her parents, Wm. E. and Nellie V. (33, 39) as well as other extended family members.

Potter, Nellie V. (36) resided with her daughter, extended family members, and her husband, Wm. E. Potter (33, 39).

Potter, Wm. E. (37) was married and worked as a book keeper. He was head of household (33. 39). He had a tax levy valued at $750 for 1 house. Mr. Potter was also the census taker in Newington for the 1880 census and was appointed as a Juror by the Town Selectmen at the 5-Jan-1880 town meeting. Mr. Potter appears to have been well respected by the residents of Newington (see the 15-Jan-1880entry in the Newington Happenings section).

Pratt, Lydia G. (63) was born in Massachusetts and married. She resided with her husband in the household of her son-in-law, Hudson H. Stoddard (46, 52). It appears she is buried in the Silver Street Cemetery in Granville, Massachusetts. The Pratt headstone there shows her as; Lydia G. / Wife Of / Wm. F. Pratt / Aug. 6, 1820 / June 27, 1891.

Pratt, Wm. F. (67) was born in New York and married. He worked as a clerk and resided with his wife in the household of his son-in-law, Hudson H. Stoddard (46, 52).

Prince, Jennie L. (18) was single and resided in the household of her brother-in-law, Geo. L. Ross (75, 82).

Quigley, Robt. A. (23) was a single farm laborer who worked in the household of Elias L. Steele (153, 161).

Quinn, Alice (10) was in school and lived with her siblings and parents, James and Mary (179, 187).

Quinn, Edward (8) lived with his siblings and parents, James and Mary (179, 187).

Quinn, James (40) was from Ireland and married. He worked as a laborer and was head of household (179, 187). His tax levy was valued at $585 which included: 1 house and 2 head of livestock.

Quinn, John (19) was single, in school, and resided with his siblings and parents, James and Mary (179, 187).

Quinn, Lucy (3 months) was born in March 1880. She lived with her siblings and parents, James and Mary (179, 187).

Quinn, Mary (40) was born in Ireland, married, and resided with her children and husband, James Quinn (179, 187).

Quinn, Mary (6) lived with her siblings and parents, James and Mary (179, 187).

Quinn, Teresa (24) was single and born in Ireland. She worked as a servant in the household of her brother-in-law, William H. Dennis (105, 112).

Quinn, William (14) was in school, and lived with his siblings and parents, James and Mary (179, 187).

Ramsey, Frank (5) lived with his siblings and mother, Hannah (61, 67).

Ramsey, Hannah (36) was widowed and born in Ireland. She worked doing washing and was head of household (61, 67). The census notes she could neither read nor write. Hannah and her family also appear on the Supplemental Schedule for the 1880 census, the entire family was listed in the pauper section.

Ramsey, John (12) was in school and lived with his siblings and mother, Hannah (61, 67).

Ramsey, Mary (13) was in school and also worked as a domestic servant. She lived with her siblings and mother, Hannah (61, 67). It would appear that Mary was also enumerated as a servant in the household of Walter F. Brown (69. 76).

Ramsey, Robert (8) was in school and lived with his siblings and mother, Hannah (61, 67). He is also noted on the census as "idiotic". Robert was also listed on the Supplemental Schedule for the 1880 census. He was labeled in the idiot section having recently been diagnosed.

Ramsey, William (11) was in school and lived with his siblings and mother, Hannah (61, 67).

Reigger, Annie (40) was married and born in Germany. She resided with her children and husband, Anton (176, 184). She is buried with her husband, in the East Cemetery in Manchester, Connecticut. The stone shows her as; His Wife / Anastasia Hitsch / 1840 – 1920.

Reigger, Anton (41) was born in Germany and married. He worked as a laborer and was head of household (176, 184). His tax levy was shown as $229 (surcharge) which included: 1 house and 6 acres of land. He is buried in the East Cemetery in Manchester, Connecticut with his wife. The headstone reads; Anton Reigger / 1838 – 1915.

Reigger, Bernard (17) was in school and lived with his siblings and parents, Anton and Annie (176, 184).

Reigger, Louise (2) lived with her siblings and parents, Anton and Annie (176, 184).

Reigger, Mary (7) lived with her siblings and parents, Anton and Annie (176, 184).

Reynolds, Bridgett (21) was married and resided with her husband, Luke Reynolds (39, 45).

Reynolds, Luke (21) was married, worked as a farm laborer, and was head of household (39, 45).

Richards, Harriet E. (34) was married and resided with her husband, Wm. M. Richards (161, 169). Harriet Elizabeth Richards died in Newington on 28-Apr-1918 at the age of 72-6-21. A burial permit was issued in Newington but no headstone has been located.

Richards, Mary J. (14) was in school and lived with her grandmother, Ann M. Deming (164, 172). The Hale Collection identifies a Mary F. Richards died Dec. 8, 1918 age 51 as being buried at the Connecticut State Hospital Cemetery in Middletown, Connecticut. This could be the same person.

Richards, Wm. E. (42) was married and worked as a farmer. He was head of household (161, 169). His tax levy was valued at $4,665 which included: 1 house, 82 acres of land, 14 head of livestock, 2 coaches and 2 clocks. A headstone in the Church Street Cemetery was noted in the Hale Collection as William M. Richards died Dec. 24, 1910 age 73. This would appear to be the same person.

Riley, David (20) was single, noted as black and worked as a farm laborer in the household of John C. Tracy (2, 3).

Riley, Thomas (35) was single and born in Ireland. He worked as a laborer in the household of Thomas Dennis (104, 111). The census noted he could not read or write.

Ring, Roe (33) was single and born in New York. He worked as a brick maker in the household of Thomas Dennis (104, 111).

Robbins, Bertha (2) lived with her parents, David L. and Catherine L. (124, 131).

Robbins, Catherine L. (26) resided with her daughter and husband, David L. Robbins (124, 131). Catherine L. Woodhouse Robbins died in Newington on 18-May-1944 aged 90-3-27 and is buried in the Newington Cemetery with her husband. The Robbins headstone shows her as; His Wife / Catherine L. Woodhouse / January 21, 1854 / May 18, 1944.

Robbins, David L. (31) was a married farmer and head of household (124, 131). His tax levy was valued at $7,874 which included: 1 clock, $1,180 in bank stock, $5,544 money at interest, and $1,100 cash on hand. David is also listed on a joint tax levy with Martin Robbins (deceased). That levy was valued at $17,826 which included: 3 houses, 381 acres of land, 39 head of livestock, and 2 coaches. The property was listed as: Home Lot – 32 ac, adj. L. Welles – 31 ac, Fifty & Chester – 95 ac, Willard – 48 ac, Bates – 10 ac, Deming – 17 ac, Hurlbut – 2 ac, North Pasture – 20 ac, River – 44 ac, Carmnon – 3 ac, Belden – 6 ac, Parsonage – 30 ac, Three Corner – 6 ac, Deming South – 27 ac, and Hubbard – 10 ac. David Lowrey Robbins, son of Lowrey and Emily, was baptized in Newington on 22-Jul-1849. He was appointed as a Juror by the Town Selectmen at the 5-Jan-1880 town meeting and later elected as Agent of the Town Deposit Fund at the meeting of 4-Oct-1880. David is buried in the Newington Cemetery with his wife, Catherine. The Robbins headstone lists him as; David L. Robbins / October 30, 1848 / January 27, 1888.

Robbins, Emily F. (65) was a widow who resided with her daughters. She was head of household (172, 180). Her tax levy was valued at $15,624 which included: $5,574 in bank stock, money at interest of $8,500, and cash on hand of $1,550. There is also a note that she has "money secured by a mortgage" of $3,000, but that amount is not included in the total value. Emily is buried in the Newington Cemetery with her husband Lowrey Robbins. The Robbins headstone lists her as; Emily F. His Wife / Born Jun. 9, 1815 / Died Oct. 20, 1881.

Robbins, Henry M. (41) was a married farmer and head of household (63, 69). His tax levy was valued at $12,871 which included: 3 houses, 212 acres of land, 39 head of livestock, 1 coach, farming utensils (valued at $100), 1 piano, and $1,680 in insurance stock. The property was known as: Home Lot – 34 ac, Blinn – 4 ac, Chester – 21 ac, B. Oak – 14 ac, adj. Blinn – 36 ac, Green Swamp – 18 ac, Kilbourne – 3 ac, S . Meadow – 2 ac, Belden – 6 ac, Griddly – 61 ac, Griswold – 1 ac, and Fitch – 12 ac. Henry Martin Robbins, son of Unni and Sarah D., was baptized in Newington on 27-Oct-1839. He was elected as a Highway Surveyor at the 4-Oct-1880 town meeting. Henry is buried in the Newington Cemetery with his wife. The Robbins stone shows him as; Henry M. Robbins / Born / Aug. 10, 1839 / Died Dec. 27, 1898.

Robbins, Lucy A. (25) was single and resided with her sister and mother, Emily F. Robbins (172, 180). Her tax levy was valued at $5,972 which included: 1 clock, 1 piano, $2,842 in bank stock, $1,400 money at interest, and $1,500 cash on hand.

Robbins, Sarah D. (75) was listed as single but was actually a widow as her husband Unni had died in 1869. She resided in the household of her son, Henry M. Robbins (63, 69). Her tax levy was valued at $400 for bank stock. Sarah is buried in the Newington Cemetery with her husband. The Robbins headstone lists her as; Sarah Dunham / His Wife / Born Jan. 7, 1805 / Died April 10, 1889.

Robbins, Sarah F. (30) was born in North Carolina and married. She resided with her children and husband, Henry M. Robbins (63, 69). Sarah died in Newington on 3-Dec-1932 aged 82-1-19 and is buried in the Newington Cemetery with her husband. The Robbins headstone lists her as; Sarah Frances / Kellogg / His Wife / Born Oct. 4, 1850 / Died Dec. 3, 1932.

Rockwell, Harriet E. (53) resided with her husband, Saml. N. Rockwell (83, 90). Harriet Eliza Kilbourne, daughter of Henry and Huldah, was baptized in Newington on 16-Sep-1827 she later married Samuel N. Rockwell there on 17-Mar-1847. The Rockwell headstone in the Newington Cemetery lists her as; Harriet E. / His Wife / Died Oct. 14, 1905 / Aged 78 Yrs.

Rockwell, Harriet W. (81) was a widow who resided in the household of her son-in-law, Walter B. Dorman (137, 143). She is buried in the Newington Cemetery with her husband, Robert. The Rockwell headstone lists her as; Harriet W. His Wife / Born / March 4, 1800 / Died / March 31, 1887.

Rockwell, Saml. N. (53) was married and worked as a joiner. He was head of household (83, 90). His tax levy was shown as $1,315 which included: 1 house and 1 head of livestock. Samuel Newton Rockwell, son of Robert and Harriet, was baptized in Newington on 18-Sep-1825 he later married Harriet Kilbourne there on 17-Mar-1847. Samuel is buried in the Newington Cemetery with his wife. The Rockwell stone shows him as; Samuel N. Rockwell / Died June 8, 1908 / Aged 83 Yrs.

Root, Eliza A. (63) was a widow who resided with her son, William A. Root (92, 99).

Root, William A. (20) was a single farm laborer and head of household (92, 99).

Rose, E. Alfred (7) was listed as being born in New Britain (typically the state or country of birth is listed. New Britain also refers to a historic name for an area near Hudson Bay in Canada) and in school. He lived with his parents, William H. and Jessie (23, 29).

Rose, Jessie (25) was born in England and resided with her son and husband, William H. Rose (23, 29). Jessie is buried in the Greenwood Cemetery in Avon, Connecticut with her husband. The Robotham family headstone lists her as; Jessie Wilson Rose / 1855 – 1898.

Rose, William H. (31) was married, born in England, and worked as an engraver. He was head of household (23, 29). He appears to be buried in the Greenwood Cemetery in Avon, Connecticut with his wife, Jessie. The Robotham family headstone shows him as; William H. Rose / 1849 – 1929.

Ross, Allie E. (9) lived with her parents, Geo. L and Mary E. (75, 82).

Ross, Geo. L. (32) was married and worked as a blacksmith. He was head of household (75, 82).

Ross, Mary E. (31) was married and resided with her daughter and husband, Geo. L. Ross (75, 82).

Rourke, James (21) was a single farm laborer who worked in the household of Emily F. Robbins (172, 180).

Rowley, Charlotte J. (50) was married and resided with her children and husband, John S. Rowley (171, 179). She is buried with her husband, in the Newington Cemetery. The headstone lists her as; Charlotte J. / His Wife / Died Nov. 5, 1895 / Aged 65 Yrs.

Rowley, Clara L. (19) lived with her siblings and parents, John S. and Charlotte J. (171, 179).

Rowley, Frank H. (10) was in school and lived with his siblings and parents, John S. and Charlotte J. (171, 179). Frank Hills Rowley died in Philadelphia, Pennsylvania on 22-Jun-1920 at the age of 50-8-16. He is buried in the Newington Cemetery with his wife, Catherine Clarke. The headstone shows him as; Frank H. Rowley / 1869 – 1920.

Rowley, Hattie I. (13) was in school and lived with her siblings and parents, John S. and Charlotte J. (171, 179).

Rowley, John S. (48) was a married farmer and head of household (171, 179). His tax levy was valued at $2,024 which included: 1 house, 49 ½ acres of land, 15 head of livestock, and 1 piano. The property was listed as: Home Lot – 18 ac, Swamp – 12 ac, Keney – 16 ac, and Rimmon – 3 ½ ac. John was elected as Collector at the 4-Oct-1880 town meeting. The headstone in the Newington Cemetery lists him as; John S. Rowley / Died May 27, 1906 / Aged 74 Yrs.

Salander, Olin (37) was born in Sweden and single. He worked as a laborer in the household of, William H. Dennis (105, 112).

Sanford, Agnes E. (26) resided with her children and husband, James A. Sanford (134, 140). She was suffering from chills and fever on the day of the census. Agnes is buried in the Fairview Cemetery in New Britain, Connecticut with her husband. The Sanford headstone lists her as; Agnes E. His Wife / 1854 – 1914.

Sanford, Alice A. (1) lived with her siblings and parents, Agnes E. and James A. (134, 140).

Sanford, James A. (30) was married and worked as a farmer. He was head of household (134, 140). His tax levy was valued at $2,337 (surcharge) which included: 1 house, 47 acres of land, and 5 head of livestock. The property was listed as: Home Lot – 25 ac, Whaples – 17 ac, and Wood – 5 ac. He is buried with his wife, Agnes, in the Fairview Cemetery in New Britain, Connecticut. The headstone shows him as; James A. Sanford / 1850 – 1923.

Sanford, Lucy A. (5) lived with her siblings and parents, Agnes E. and James A. (134, 140). She is buried with her parents in the Fairview Cemetery in New Britain, Connecticut and is shown on the Sanford stone as; Lucy Sanford O'Day / 1875 – 1967.

Sanford, Rollin (28) was single and worked as a pattern maker. He resided with the family of his brother, James A. Sanford (134, 140). There was a tax levy for an R.S. Sanford that was valued at $22 (surcharge) for 1 head of livestock. This could be the same person.

Scally, John (35) was born in Ireland and single. He worked as a farm laborer in the household of Marcus L. Stoddard (20, 26).

Scanlon, John (9) lived with his siblings and parents, Thos. and Mary (29, 35).

Scanlon, Mary (38) was from Ireland and married. She resided with her children and husband, Thos. Scanlon (29, 35). The census noted that she could neither read nor write.

Scanlon, Nellie (7) lived with her siblings and parents, Thos. and Mary (29, 35).

Scanlon, Thomas (4) lived with his siblings and parents, Thos. and Mary (29, 35).

Scanlon, Thos. (40) was born in Ireland and married. He worked as a laborer and was head of household (29, 35). His tax levy was valued at $506 which included: 1 house, 1 acre of land, and 1 head of livestock.

Screen, Alfred (21) was born in Massachusetts and married. He worked as a farm laborer and was head of household (117, 124).

Screen, Lydia (19) resided with her husband, Alfred Screen (117, 124).

Seymour, Abigail W. (54) was married and resided with her sons and husband, John D. Seymour (17, 22). Abigail Welles, daughter of Roger and Electa, was baptized in Newington on 4-Jun-1826 and later married John D. Seymour there on 25-Nov-1852. She is buried with her husband in the Newington Cemetery, their headstone reads; Abigail Welles / His Wife / 1825 – 1901.

Seymour, Geo. W. (14) was in school and lived with his brother and parents, John D. and Abigail W. (17, 22). George Wolcott Seymour was baptized on 28-Jun-1866 in Newington. He is buried with his wife, Rose, in the Johnson Chapel Cemetery in Confluence, Pennsylvania. The Seymour headstone lists him as; George W. / 1865 – 1943.

Seymour, John D. (58) was married and worked as a farmer. He was head of household (17, 22). His tax levy was valued at $6,003 which included: 2 houses, 103 ½ acres of land, 14 head of livestock, and 1 piano. The property was noted as: Home Lot – 6 ac, West – 76 ac, Davenport – 13 ac, and Kilbourne – 8 ½ ac. He married Abigail Welles in Newington on 25-Nov-1852 and died there on 24-Dec-1903 aged 82-3-22. The Hale Collection notes his burial in Newington Cemetery as; John Deming Seymour 1821 – 1903.

Seymour, William W. (20) was listed as a student who resided with his brother and parents, John D. and Abigail W. (17, 22). He was baptized in Newington on 23-Sep-1860. William is buried in the Parkholm Cemetery in La Grange Park, Illinois. His stone reads; William Seymour / Oct. 6, 1859 / Dec. 11, 1951.

Shelden, Charles E. (17) was in school and also worked as a clerk in an office (probably with his father). He lived with his siblings and parents, Edward C. and Ellen J. (11, 14).

Shelden, Edward C. (44) was born in England and married. He worked as a real estate broker and was head of household (11, 14). His tax levy was valued at $110 (surcharge) which included: 1 watch and 1 organ. Edward Shelton was appointed as a Juror at the town meeting on 5-Jan-1880. This is likely the same individual.

Shelden, Ellen J. (42) resided with her children and husband, Edward C. Shelden (11, 14).

Shelden, Mable E. (14) was in school and lived with her siblings and parents, Edward C. and Ellen J. (11, 14).

Shelden, Wilbur N. (8) lived with his siblings and parents, Edward C. and Ellen J. (11, 14).

Simcox, John (14) was born in Ireland and worked as a farm laborer in the household of Peter Byrne (129, 136).

Smart, Harriet (see Dee, William Mrs.)

Smith, Burt (28) was from New York, single and worked as a farm laborer in the household of, John S. Kirkham (94, 101).

Smith, Caroline (61) resided with her daughters and husband, Leander Smith (28, 34). Caroline Huntley, of Ellington, Connecticut, married Leander Smith on 4-Jul-1841 in Newington.

Smith, Leander (62) was married and worked as a farm laborer. He was head of household (28, 34). His tax levy was valued at $110 (surcharge) for one house. He married Caroline Huntley, of Ellington, Connecticut in Newington on 4-Jul-1841.

Smith, Mary (36) was single and resided with her sister and parents, Leander and Caroline (28, 34).

Smith, Mattie (13) was in school and lived with her sister and parents, Leander and Caroline (28, 34). Mattie may actually be the daughter of Mary Smith in the same household.

Smith, Theodore (45) was single and worked as a shoemaker. He lived alone in household (45, 51).

Spencer, Jerusha (57) was listed as divorced. She worked as a housekeeper in the household of Hiram E. Stoddard (42, 48).

Squires, Betsey (73) was a widow who lived alone in household (139, 145). Her tax levy was valued at $55 (surcharge) for one house. Betsey was also listed on the Supplemental Schedule for the 1880 census in the pauper section with the disability of "old age". Betsey Squires, of Wethersfield, Connecticut, married Stephen Tando in Newington on 16-May-1827. If this is same person it appears that she returned to using her maiden name at some point after she became a widow.

Starr, Edmund (15) was in school and lived with his siblings and parents, Jared and Emma R. (102, 109).

Starr, Elsie G. (6) lived with her siblings and parents, Jared and Emma R. (102, 109). She is buried in the Cedar Grove Cemetery in New London, Connecticut. Her headstone reads; Elsie G. Starr / 1874 – 1958.

Starr, Emma H. (18) was single and resided with her siblings and parents, Jared and Emma R. (102, 109). She is buried with other family members in the Cedar Grove Cemetery in New London, Connecticut. Her stone reads; Emma Hall Starr / Dec. 24, 1861 – Feb. 10, 1890.

Starr, Emma R. (46) resided with her children and husband, Jared Starr (102, 109). Her obituary in the Hartford Courant indicates she died at her home in Newington and the funeral was held at Grace Church there. Emma is buried with her husband, in the Cedar Grove Cemetery in New London, Connecticut. The headstone lists her as; Emma R. Starr / Died Dec. 15, 1915 / AE 82.

Starr, Frederick W. (12) was in school and lived with his siblings and parents, Jared and Emma R. (102, 109). It appears he may be buried in the Wilcox Cemetery in Berlin, Connecticut. A headstone there reads; Frederick W. Starr / 1868 – 1947.

Starr, Jared (45) was married and worked as a farmer. He was head of household (102, 109). His tax levy was valued at $3,536 (surcharge) which included: 2 houses, 45 acres of land, 9 head of livestock, 2 clocks and 1 piano. The property was identified as: Meadow Lot – 1 ac, Middle – 8 ac, and East – 36 ac. Jared was appointed as a Juror by the Town Selectmen at the 5-Jan-1880 town meeting and later elected as an Auditor and Hayward (Town official in charge of fences and enclosures) at the meeting of 4-Oct-1880. He is buried with his wife, Emma, in the Cedar Grove Cemetery in New London, Connecticut. The headstone shows him as; Jared Starr / Died June 27, 1924 / AE 89.

Starr, Jonathan (21) was single and worked as a bookkeeper. He resided with his siblings and parents, Jared and Emma R. (102, 109). Jonathan also served as a State Republican delegate (see the 4-Aug-1880 entry in the Newington Happenings section). He appears to have died in 1917 and is buried in the Cedar Grove Cemetery in New London, Connecticut.

Steele, Alonzo W. (52) was married and worked as a farmer. He was head of household (145, 151).

Steele, Daisy O. (7) lived with her siblings and parents, Saml. A and Matilda (180, 188).

Steele, Elias L. (36) was single, worked as a lawyer, and was head of household (153, 161). His tax levy was valued at $1,226 which included: 1 house, 29 acres of land, and 6 head of livestock. The property was listed as: Home Lot – 12 ac, Whaples – 5 ac, Deming – 10 ac, and Andrus – 2 ac. Elias is listed as a conservator on another tax levy valued at $1,500 for 50 acres of land. He was elected as a Justice of the Peace at the 8-Nov-1880 town meeting. Elias is buried in the Beckley Cemetery in Berlin, Connecticut. The headstone shows him as; Elias M. Steele / Died Dec. 10, 1897 / Aged 53.

Steele, Ella (11) was in school and lived with her siblings and parents, Alonzo W. and Mary E. (145, 151).

Steele, Eva J. (15) was in school and lived with her siblings and parents, Alonzo W. and Mary E. (145, 151).

Steele, Harry J. (3) lived with his parents, Joel and Martha L. (157, 165). He is buried with his parents in the East Avon Cemetery in Avon, Connecticut. The headstone lists him as; Their Son / Harry J. Steele / 1877 – 1930.

Steele, Henry D. (9) lived with his siblings and parents, Alonzo W. and Mary E. (145, 151).

Steele, Isse (1) lived with her siblings and parents, Alonzo W. and Mary E. (145, 151).

Steele, Joel (37) was married and worked as a farmer. He was head of household (157, 165). Joel is buried with his family in the East Avon Cemetery in Avon, Connecticut. The Steele family headstone shows him as; Joel Steele / 1838 – 1914.

Steele, John R. (21) was born in New Jersey and resided with his siblings and parents, Saml. A. and Matilda (180, 188). John was single and worked as a farm laborer.

Steele, Marilla L. (24) was single and worked as a school teacher. She resided with her siblings and parents, Saml. A. and Matilda (180, 188).

Steele, Martha L. (28) resided with her son and husband, Joel Steele (157, 165). She is buried with her husband, in the East Avon Cemetery in Avon, Connecticut. The Steele stone lists her as; His Wife / Martha L. Rodgers / 1850 – 1928.

Steele, Mary E. (40) resided with her children and husband, Alonzo W. Steele (145, 151).

Steele, Matilda (42) was from New York and resided with her children and husband, Saml. A. Steele (180, 188).

Steele, Nellie M. (15) was born in New York and attended school. She lived with her siblings and parents, Saml. A. and Matilda (180, 188).

Steele, Rosa J. (5) lived with her siblings and parents, Alonzo W. and Mary E. (145, 151).

Steele, Saml. A. (51) was married and worked as a farmer. He was head of household (180, 188). His tax levy was valued at $3,523 which included: 1 house, 89 acres of land, and 3 head of livestock. The property was listed as: Home Lot – 44 ac, Mountain – 39 ac, and Parsonage – 6 ac. Samuel was appointed as a Juror by the Town Selectmen at the 5-Jan-1880 town meeting and later elected as a Justice of the Peace at the 8-Nov-1880 meeting.

Steele, Waldo S. (9) was in school and lived with his siblings and parents, Saml. A. and Matilda (180, 188).

Sternberg, Annie B. (11) was born in California and attended school. She lived with her siblings and parents, John C. and Mary A. (7, 10).

Sternberg, Fanny S. (7) lived with her siblings and parents, John C. and Mary A. (7, 10). The Hale Collection notes her burial in Spring Grove Cemetery in Hartford, Connecticut. She is listed as; Francesca S. Sternberg Davis wife of G.F., born 27-Jun-1873 died 19-Feb-1902.

Sternberg, John C. (42) was born in Germany and married. He worked as the postmaster and was head of household (7, 10). He also served as a Republican delegate from Newington (see the 1-Apr-1880 entry in the Newington Happenings section). The Hale Collection lists his burial in the Fairview Cemetery in West Hartford, Connecticut. He is shown in Lot-94 as John G. Sternberg 1838 – 1896 with a Civil War flag marker.

Sternberg, John C. Jr. (4) lived with his siblings and parents, John C. and Mary A. (7, 10). He is buried in the Cavalry Cemetery in Waterbury, Connecticut. The Sternberg stone lists him as; John C. Sternberg / Died Aug. 29, 1933 / Age 57 Yrs.

Sternberg, Katie E. (12) was born in California and attended school. She lived with her siblings and parents, John C. and Mary A. (7, 10).

Sternberg, Mary A. (31) resided with her children and husband, John C. Sternberg (7, 10). She is buried with her husband in Lot-94 of the Fairview Cemetery in West Hartford, Connecticut and is listed as Mary A. Sternberg wife of John G. 1849 – 1907.

Stevens, David (66) was listed as married but no wife was with him. He resided with his son, Frank W. Stevens (149, 155).

Stevens, Eliza (28) was from New York and resided with her husband, Frank W. Stevens (149, 155). She is buried with her husband, in the Beckley Cemetery in Berlin, Connecticut. The headstone reads; His Wife / Eliza Seaker / 1851 – 1936.

Stevens, Frank W. (28) was married and worked as a farmer. He was head of household (149, 155). Frank is buried with his wife, in the Beckley Cemetery in Berlin, Connecticut. The headstone reads; Frank Stevens / 1850 – 1937.

Stoddard, Arthur W. (13) was in school and lived with his siblings and mother, Sarah W. Stoddard (19, 25). Arthur Winthrop Stoddard, son of Rufus and Sarah, was baptized in Newington on 5-May-1867. He is buried in the Lewiston City Cemetery in Lewiston, Montana. The headstone reads; Arthur W. Stoddard / 2 Lieut. / 1 Mont. Inf. / Sp. Am. War.

Stoddard, Caroline S. (54) was from Massachusetts and resided with her husband John G. Stoddard (1, 1). She is buried in the Newington Cemetery alongside her husband. Her stone reads; Caroline S. / 1825 – 1905.

Stoddard, Carrie S. (23) resided with her children and husband, Marcus L. Stoddard (20, 26). Caroline Francis Stoddard died in West Hartford, Connecticut on 5-May-1950 at the age of 93. She is buried in the Newington Cemetery with her husband, Marcus and other family members.

Stoddard, Elma A. (29) resided with her children and husband, Hudson H. Stoddard (46, 52). She appears to be buried in the Kearney Cemetery in Kearney, Nebraska. Her headstone reads; Elma A. / Stoddard / 1850 – 1938.

Stoddard, Emily W. (23) resided with her siblings and widowed mother, Sarah W. Stoddard (19, 25). Emily Welles Stoddard, daughter of Rufus and Sarah, was baptized in Newington on 26-Apr-1857.

Stoddard, Frances S. (62) was a widow and resided with the family of her son, Marcus L. Stoddard (20, 26). Her tax levy was valued at $5,211 (the total in the ledger is shown as $5,221, there appears to be an addition error of $10) items included were: 1 clock and $4,697 in bank stock. Frances is buried with her husband, Marcus W., in the Newington Cemetery. The stone shows her as; Frances S. / His Wife / Born / June 5, 1817 / Died / Mar. 21, 1901.

Stoddard, Frank R. (18) was single and worked as a farm laborer. He resided with his siblings and widowed mother, Sarah W. Stoddard (19, 25). Frank Rufus Stoddard, son of Rufus and Sarah, was baptized in Newington on 25-Sep-1861. Frank apparently died in Martinsdale, Montana and is buried in the Newington Cemetery with family members. The stone lists him as; Frank R. Stoddard / Died Jan. 26, 1891 / Aged 29 Yrs.

Stoddard, Hepsie (53) was single and resided with her nephew, Chas. J. Wells (119, 126). She should have been noted as a widow rather than single. Hepsebath Deming, daughter of Jedediah (no mother listed), was baptized in Newington on 27-Mar-1827 and married Charles Stoddard there on 14-Dec-1853. Her tax levy was valued at $3,615 which included: $1,615 in bank stock and $2000 money at interest. Her headstone in the Newington Cemetery reads; Hepzibah Deming / Wife Of / Charles Stoddard / Born / Feb. 27, 1827 / Died / Mar. 17, 1896.

Stoddard, Hiram E. (82) was a widowed farmer and head of household (42, 48). His tax levy was shown as $1,800 which included: 1 house, 44 acres of land, and 4 head of livestock. The property was listed as: Woodbridge – 5 ac, Home Lot – 2 ac, Swamp – 7 ac, Hill – 11 ac, and West – 19 ac. Hiram Edwards Stoddard, son of Jonathan and Candace, was baptized in Newington on 14-Jun-1812. He seems to have died in 1883 and is buried in the Newington Cemetery with other family members.

Stoddard, Hudson H. (42) was a married publisher and head of household (46, 52). He had a tax levy valued at $1,808 which included: 1 house, ½ acre of land, 1 head of livestock, 2 coaches, and 1 piano. Hiram Hudson Stoddard, son of Hiram E. and Fanny, was baptized in Newington on 22-Oct-1837. He is buried in the Kearney Cemetery in Kearney, Nebraska. His stone reads; Hiram H. Stoddard / Co. C / 5 Conn. Inf. / 1837 – 1922.

Stoddard, John G. (52) was a married farmer who was head of household (1, 1). His tax levy was valued at $2,445 which included: 1 house, 21 acres of land, 7 head of livestock, 1 organ and $50 money at interest. The property was known as: Home Lot – 2 ac, Day – 6 ac, East – 10 ac, and Dirt Swamp – 3 ac. John Gaylord Stoddard, son of Hiram E. and Fanny, was baptized in Newington on 18-May-1828. He was elected as a Grand Juror at the town meeting of 4-Oct-1880. The Hale Collection notes his burial in the Newington Cemetery and is listed as; John G. Stoddard 1828 – 1913. Also see the entry dated 17-Sep-1880 in the Newington Happenings section for a classified ad.

Stoddard, John R. (24) was married and worked as a farm laborer. He resided in the home of his father, John G. Stoddard, but was head of his own household (1, 2). John was elected as a Registrar of Voters at the town meeting of 4-Oct-1880. John Roswell Stoddard died on 3-Jan-1936 in Newington aged 80-5-28. He is buried in the Newington Cemetery with other Stoddard family members. His stone reads; John R. / 1855 – 1936.

Stoddard, Lila M. (25) was from New York and resided with her daughter and husband, John R. Stoddard (1, 2). Lila Steele Stoddard died in Hartford, Connecticut on 18-Apr-1943 aged 88-6-4. She is buried in the Newington Cemetery with other Stoddard family members. Her stone reads; Ella M. / 1854 – 1943.

Stoddard, Louis A. (2) lived with his siblings and parents, Marcus L. and Carrie S. (20, 26). He died shortly after the census was taken (see the entry dated 23-Sep-1880 in the Newington Happenings section) and is buried in the Newington Cemetery with his parents. The Stoddard stone lists him as; Lewis Allen / Died Sept. 21, 1880 / Aged 2 yrs. 4 mos.

Stoddard, Louise B. (1) lived with her parents, John R. and Lila M. (1, 2).

Stoddard, Lynn F. (4) lived with his siblings and parents, Hudson H. and Elma A. (46, 52). He is buried in Fairhaven Memorial Park in Santa Ana, California. His stone reads; Husband & Father / Lynn F. Stoddard / 1875 – 1945.

Stoddard, Marcus L. (25) was a married farmer and head of household (20, 26). His tax levy was shown as $4,437 which included: 2 houses, 88 acres of land, and 17 head of livestock. Marcus Lewis Stoddard, son of Marcus W. and Frances S, was baptized in Newington on 31-Dec-1854. At the 18-Oct-1880 town meeting he was appointed by the selectmen as a Deputy Registrar of Voters. He also served as a Republican delegate from Newington (see the 1-Apr-1880 in the Newington Happenings section). Marcus is buried with other Stoddard family members in the Newington Cemetery. The Stoddard headstone lists him as; Marcus Lewis Stoddard / Born July 22, 1854 / Died Feb. 16, 1917.

Stoddard, Sadie L. (1) was shown as this age but was born in April 1880. She lived with her siblings and parents, Hudson H. and Elma A. (46, 52).

Stoddard, Sarah W. (50) was listed as both married and widowed on the census but no spouse is shown in the household. She resided with her children and was head of household (19, 25). Sarah is buried in the Newington Cemetery with her husband, Rufus. The Stoddard stone shows her as; Sarah Wells / His Wife / Born June 27, 1827 / Died April 29, 1894.

Stoddard, (un-named) (2 mos. old) was a daughter born in March. She lived with her siblings and parents, Marcus L. and Carrie S. (20, 26). This would appear to be Gertrude F. Stoddard. She is buried with her husband, Charles W. Belden, in the Newington Cemetery. The Belden headstone lists her as; Gertrude F. Stoddard / His Wife / Mar. 16, 1880 – Nov. 6, 1923.

Stotzer, Delia (22) was single and worked as a servant in the household of Franklin C. Latimer (168, 176). She is buried in the Newington Cemetery and the headstone reads; Delia Stotzer / Died / Aug. 18, 1907 / Aged 49 Yrs. She was likely the daughter of Ernst and Mary E. Stotzer (140, 146).

Stotzer, Ernst (51) was from Germany, married, and worked as a farmer. He was head of household (140, 146). His tax levy was valued at $1,704 which included: 1 house, 41 acres of land, and 10 head of livestock. The property was known as: Home Lot – 8 ac, Hill – 12 ac, Pasture – 18 ac, and West – 3 ac. His headstone in the Newington Cemetery reads; Ernst Stotzer / Died Apr. 1, 1905 / Aged 76 Yrs.

Stotzer, Ernst (16) was in school and worked as a farm laborer. He lived with his siblings and parents, Ernst and Mary E. (140, 146). There is an Ernest Stotzer, who died in 1945, buried in the Saint Mary Cemetery in New Britain, Connecticut which could be this individual.

Stotzer, Frank (18) was a single farm laborer who worked in the household of, John S. Rowley (171, 179). There was a burial permit issued for Frank Stotzer who died in Hartford, Connecticut on 26-Jun-1945 aged 81-7-30. No grave was located in Newington for this individual and the permit seems to be for this person. It is also likely that Frank was the son of Ernst and Mary E. Stotzer (140, 146).

Stotzer, Lydia (12) was in school and lived with her siblings and parents, Ernst and Mary E. (140, 146). She is buried in the Newington Cemetery and her headstone reads; Lydia Stotzer / Born / Sept. 2, 1867 / Died / March 11, 1884.

Stotzer, Mary E. (49) was born in Germany and married. She resided with her children and husband, Ernst Stotzer (140, 146). The Hale Collection shows her burial in the Newington Cemetery as, Mary E. Stotzer wife of Ernst died Feb. 21, 1897 aged 66 y. There is headstone there with the matching date and age, but the given name is illegible.

Stotzer, Mary E. (79) was born in Germany and a widow. She resided with the family of her son, Ernst Stotzer (140, 146). Mary is buried in the Newington Cemetery and her headstone reads; Mary E. Stotzer / Born / Jan. 4, 1801 / Died / June 26, 1885.

Stotzer, Robert (18) was single and worked as a farm laborer. He resided with his siblings and parents, Ernst and Mary E. (140, 146). His headstone in the Newington Cemetery reads; Robert Stotzer / Born / Oct. 27, 1862 / Died / March 5, 1884.

Sullivan, James (28) was single and from Ireland. He worked as a laborer in the household of William H. Dennis (105, 112).

Sullivan, Matthew (22) was single and from Ireland. He worked as a laborer in the household of William H. Dennis (105, 112).

Talina, Rudolph (18) was a single laborer from Sweden. He worked in the household of Levi G. Clark (80, 87).

Taylor, Margaret (87) was a widow from Massachusetts who resided in the household of her son-in-law, William Hubbard (76, 83). She had a tax levy that was valued at $300 for 1 house. Margaret died shortly after the census was taken and is buried in the Newington Cemetery. Her headstone reads; Margaret / Widow Of / Roland Taylor / Died / Dec. 8, 1880 / AE 88.

Thrasher, Chas. W. (25) was a married farm laborer who was head of household (64, 70). His tax levy was valued at $159 (surcharge) which included: 1 house and 2 head of livestock. His headstone in the Newington Cemetery reads; Charles M. Thrasher / Born / Apr. 22, 1855 / Died June 26, 1887.

Thrasher, Edith (2) lived with her sister and parents, Chas. W. and Martha (64, 70). She is buried with her mother, in the Fairview Cemetery in New Britain, Connecticut. The Thrasher stone lists her as; Edith T. Burgar / 1877 – 1955. A separate stone shows her as; Edith Thrasher / Wife Of / Fred E. Burgar / 1877 – 1955.

Thrasher, Martha (27) was married and resided with her children and husband, Chas. W. Thrasher (64, 70). She is buried with two of her children in the Fairview Cemetery in New Britain, Connecticut. The Thrasher headstone lists her as; Martha C. Thrasher / 1853 – 1924.

Thrasher, Nellie M. (5) lived with her sister and parents, Chas. W. and Martha (64, 70). She is buried with her husband, Edward Hanson, in the Fairview Cemetery in New Britain, Connecticut. The Hanson stone shows her as; Nellie M. Thrasher / His Wife / 1875 – 1966.

Tobin, Ellen (45) was from Ireland and single. She worked as a servant in the household of Marcus L. Stoddard (20, 26). The census notes she could neither read nor write.

Toomey, Patrick (33) was single and from Ireland. He worked as a laborer in the household of William H. Dennis (105, 112).

Torpy, Michael (35) was a single laborer from Ireland. He worked in the household of Thomas Dennis (104, 111). The census notes he could not read or write.

Tracy, Ada C. (12) was in school and lived with her siblings and parents, John C. and L. Louise (2, 3).

Tracy, Agnes M. (16) was in school and lived with her siblings and parents, John C. and L. Louise (2, 3). Her headstone in the Spring Grove Cemetery in Hartford, Connecticut reads; Agnes M. Tracy / 1863 – 1946.

Tracy, Frederick P. (15) was in school and lived with his siblings and parents, John C. and L. Louise (2, 3). His headstone in the Cedar Hill Cemetery in Hartford, Connecticut reads; Frederick P. Tracy / 1864 – 1915.

Tracy, Genevieve (7) lived with her siblings and parents, John C. and L. Louise (2, 3).

Tracy, Hubert D. (13) was in school and lived with his siblings and parents, John C. and L. Louise (2, 3). He is buried in the Cedar Hill Cemetery in Hartford, Connecticut, his headstone reads; Hubert D. Tracy / 1866 – 1937.

Tracy, John C. (50) was a married bookkeeper and head of household (2, 3). His tax levy was valued at $220 (surcharge) for 7 head of livestock. The headstone in the Spring Grove Cemetery in Hartford, Connecticut shows him as; John C. Tracy / 1830 – 1905.

Tracy, L. Louise (49) was married and resided with her children and husband, John C. Tracy (2, 3). She is buried in the Spring Grove Cemetery in Hartford, Connecticut. Her headstone reads; L. Louise Adams / Wife Of / John C. Tracy / 1830 – 1920.

Tracy, Louis A. (21) was single and worked as a bank clerk. He resided with his siblings and parents, John C. and L. Louise (2, 3). Louis is buried with his wife, Mary, in the Cedar Hill Cemetery in Hartford, Connecticut. The Tracy stone lists him as; Louis Adams Tracy / 1858 – 1935.

Tracy, Sophia L. (52) resided with her husband, Thomas, in the in household of her mother, Sophia Kirkham (95, 102). Sophia L. Kirkham married Thomas Tracy, of New Britain, Connecticut in Newington on 13-Jun-1872 and later died there on 3-Jun-1904 at the age of 75-9. The Hale Collection lists her burial in the Newington Cemetery as; Sofia L. Kirkham Tracy wife of Thomas, born Sept. 3, 1828 died June 3, 1904.

Tracy, Thomas (70) worked as a machinist and lived with his wife in the household of his mother-in-law, Sophia Kirkham (95, 102). He married Sophia L. Kirkham on 13-Jun-1872 in Newington.

Treall, Aurore (35) was from Canada and married. She resided with her children and husband, Joseph (108, 115). The census noted she could not read or write. The Hale Collection shows her buried in the Mount Saint Benedict Cemetery in Bloomfield, Connecticut. She is noted as Aurora Treall 1847 – 1910.

Treall, Caroline (5) lived with her sister and parents, Joseph and Aurore (108, 115).

Treall, Cordelia (3) lived with her sister and parents, Joseph and Aurore (108, 115).

Treall, Joseph (34) was a laborer from Canada. He was married and head of household (108, 115). The Hale Collection shows him buried in the Mount Saint Benedict Cemetery in Bloomfield, Connecticut, as Joseph Treall 1848 – 1930.

Trude: Both Arthur and Esther are enumerated in two different households on this census. First as the in-laws of Wm. E. Potter (33, 39) and secondly in their own household (79, 86). Their ages and occupations differ in each case but it would seem that these are in fact the same people. It does seem odd that they would have been counted twice especially since Wm. E. Potter was the census taker and was related by marriage to both Esther and Andrew. I have listed both sets of Arthur and Esther as they appear in the record.

Trude, Arthur M. (22) was a single laborer that resided in the household of his brother-in-law; Wm. E. Potter (33, 39).

Trude, Arthur W. (23) was a single sewing machine agent. He resided with his widowed mother; Esther A. Trude (79, 86).

Trude, Esther A. (68) was a widow residing with the family of her son-in-law; Wm. E. Potter (33, 39).

Trude, Esther A. (66) was a widow who resided with her son. She was head of household (79, 86).

Urlgus, Flora L. (35) was from Massachusetts and married. She resided with her husband, Henry Urlgus (122, 129).

Urlgus, Henry (45) was from England and worked as a mechanic. He was married and head of household (122, 129).

Vami, William (29) was a single laborer from Ireland. He worked in the household of Thomas Dennis (104, 111).

Vest, Lena (64) was from Germany and single, she resided with the family of her nephew, Peter Christiansen (27, 33). The census noted she could neither read nor write.

Warner, Frances A. (34) was a widow who resided with her sister and mother, Emily F. Robbins (172, 180). Her tax levy was shown as $2,794 (surcharge) which included: $2,400 in bank stock and $140 money at interest. Frances Arabella Robbins, daughter of Lowrey and Emily, was baptized in Newington on 19-Jul-1846 and later died there on 7-Oct-1904 at the age of 59-4-4. Frances is buried in the Newington Cemetery with her husband, Oliver. The Warner headstone lists her as; Frances A. Robbins / His Wife / Died Oct. 7, 1904 / AE 59.

Waterman, Geo. M. (26) was a single farm laborer who worked in the household of Franklin C. Latimer (168, 176).

Webster, Chester C. (46) was widowed and resided with his children and was head of household (152, 160). He had no occupation noted. Chester had married Marilla Richards in Newington on 3-May-1852. Marilla died in 1912 so it is unclear as to why Chester was noted as widowed on the census. She does not appear in Newington on the 1880 census. Perhaps they were actually separated, divorced or she was visiting relatives or friends elsewhere. There is a headstone for Charles C. Webster in the Newington Cemetery but the dates are mostly illegible.

Webster, Frances (Hattie) E. (24) was noted as Frances but also has the name Hattie written above it. She was single and resided with her siblings and parents, John and Lydia (159, 167).

Webster, John (60) was a married farmer and head of household (159, 167). His tax levy was valued at $7,624 which included: 1 house, 162 acres of land, 33 head of livestock, 47 sheep, 1 coach, and 1 piano. The property was known as: Home Farm – 120 ac, Kelsey – 13 ac, Ellis – 10 ac, Rimmon – 4 ac (20 ac transferred to Doherwent by the Board of Relief), Chester – 13 ac, and Francis – 2 ac. John was elected as a Hayward (Town official in charge of fences and enclosures) and Highway Surveyor at the 4-Oct-1880 town meeting. He is buried in the Beckley Cemetery in Berlin, Connecticut with his wife Lydia. His headstone reads; John Webster / Born / Dec. 20, 1818 / Died Feb. 17, 1897.

Webster, Joseph (23) was single and from New York. He worked as a farm laborer in the household of Chester C. Webster (152, 160). There is no indication if they are related. The census noted he could not read or write.

Webster, Lydia (58) was from Massachusetts, married and resided with her children and husband, John Webster (159, 167). She is buried with her husband, in the Beckley Cemetery in Berlin, Connecticut. The stone shows her as; Lydia Francis / His Wife / Born Nov. 5, 1821 / Died Oct. 25, 1906.

Webster, Minnie (17) lived with her siblings and parents, John and Lydia (159, 167).

Webster, Nellie M. (23) was single and worked as a school teacher. She resided with her brother and father, Chester C. Webster (152, 160). Nellie Marilla Webster died in Hartford, Connecticut on 4-Mar-1945 aged 88-1-5, and is buried in the Newington Cemetery. The stone shows her as; Nellie M. / Daughter / 1857 – 1945.

Webster, Oliver R. (25) was single and worked as a farmer. He resided with his sister and father, Chester C. Webster (152, 160). Oliver is buried in the Newington Cemetery with his wife, Nellie Weir (144, 150). The headstone lists him as; Oliver Webster / 1855 – 1910.

Webster, Sylvester (90) was widowed and head of household (160, 168). He is buried in the Beckley Cemetery in Berlin, Connecticut and the Webster headstone there lists him as; Sylvester Webster / Died / Aug. 16, 1883 / AE. 93.

Webster, William (26) was a single farmer who resided with his siblings and parents; John and Lydia (159, 167).

Weir, George L. (5) lived with his siblings and parents, Wellmon B. and Susan S. (144, 150). He may be buried in the Fairview Cemetery in New Britain, Connecticut.

Weir, Lucy A. (13) was in school and lived with her siblings and parents, Wellmon B. and Susan S. (144, 150).

Weir, Mary A. (66) was a widow who lived alone in household (143, 149). Her headstone in the Newington Cemetery reads; Mary Ann Churchill / Wife Of / Flavel Weir / Born Apr. 26, 1814 / Died Dec. 11, 1893 / Aged 79.

Weir, Nellie G. (11) was in school and lived with her siblings and parents, Wellmon B. and Susan S. (144, 150). She is buried with her husband, Oliver Webster (152, 160), in the Newington Cemetery, their headstone lists her as; Nellie V. Weir / His Wife / 1868 – 1893.

Weir, Susan S. (39) resided with her children and husband, Wellmon B. Weir (144, 150). She is buried in the Newington Cemetery and her stone reads; Susan S. / Wife Of / Wellman B. Weir / Died May 12, 1920 / AE 81.

Weir, Wellmon B. (40) was a married farmer and head of household (144, 150). His headstone in the Newington Cemetery reads; Wellman B. Weir / Co. B 22 Inf. / Conn. Vols. / Died Feb. 9, 1910 / AE 71.

Weirs, Clarissa H. (62) was a widow who resided with her children and was head of household (135, 141). She is buried in the Newington Cemetery with her husband, Truman. The headstone shows her as; Clarissa His Wife / Died / June 6, 1889 / Aged 71.

Weirs, Mary E. (39) was single and resided with her brother and mother; Clarissa H. Weirs (135, 141). She is buried in the Newington Cemetery with her family. The Weirs headstone lists her as; Children / M. Elizabeth Weirs / Died / Feb. 23, 1908 / Aged 67.

Weirs, Truman F. (41) was single and worked as a farmer. He resided with his sister and mother; Clarissa H. Weirs (135, 141). His tax levy was valued at $395 which included: 1 house and 4 head of livestock. Truman is buried in the Newington Cemetery with his parents and sister. The headstone lists him as; Children / Truman F. Weirs / Died / Dec. 22, 1900 / Aged 61.

Welch, John (22) was from Canada and single. He worked as a farm laborer in the household of John D. Seymour (17, 22).

Welles, Edwin S. (13) was in school and lived with his siblings and parents, Roger and Mercy D. (88 95). Edwin Stanley Welles was baptized in Newington on 10-Mar-1867. He died in Hartford, Connecticut on 2-Jan-1949, aged 82-3-27, and is buried in the Newington Cemetery. His headstone there reads; Edwin Stanley / Welles / Sept. 5, 1866 – Jan. 2, 1949.

Welles, Edwin (62) was a married farmer who was head of household (58, 64). His tax levy was shown as $4,360 which included: 2 houses, 72 acres of land, and 20 head of livestock. The property was listed as: Home Lot – 2 ac, Latimer – 32 ac, Plain – 33 ac, and Mountain – 5 ac. Edwin was also the executor of the estate of his father, Roger Welles, which had its own tax levy shown as $1,575 which included: 36 acres of land known as the Belden Lot and $675 in bank stock. Edwin, son of Roger and Electa, was baptized in Newington on 19-Aug-1821. He later married in Newington, Lucy L. Robbins, on 16-Jan-1853. Edwin was appointed Chairman for the town meeting on 19-Aug-1880. He is buried with his wife in the Newington Cemetery. The Welles headstone lists him as; Edwin Welles / Born Mar. 29, 1818 / Died Feb. 2, 1908.

Welles, Electa S. (84) was a widow who resided in the household of her son, Roger Welles (88, 95). She died shortly after the census and is buried in the Newington Cemetery. Her headstone reads; Electa Stanley / Relict Of / Roger Welles / Born / July 14, 1796 / Died / Oct. 25, 1880.

Welles, Fanny A. (26) was single and resided with her sister and parents; Edwin and Lucy L. (58, 64). Fanny Augusta Welles was baptized on 21-May-1854 in Newington. She later died in Hartford, Connecticut on 3-Nov-1919 at the age of 65-10-30. The Hale Collection shows her burial in the Newington Cemetery as; Fanny Augusta Welles Dec. 4, 1853 – Nov. 3, 1919.

Welles, Grace M. (6) lived with her siblings and parents; Roger and Mercy D. (88, 95). Grace is buried in the Newington Cemetery and her headstone reads; Grace Welles / Beadle / May 12, 1874 – Oct. 27, 1954.

Welles, Lemuel A. (9) lived with his siblings and parents; Roger and Mercy D. (88, 95). Lemuel Aikin Welles was baptized in Newington on 26-Mar-1871. He died in 1953 and is buried in the Maple Shade Cemetery in Ridgefield, Connecticut.

Welles, Lucy L. (50) was married and resided with her children and husband; Edwin Welles (58, 64). Lucy Lowrey Robbins, daughter of Unni and Sarah, was baptized in Newington on 25-May-1829 and later married Edwin Welles there on 16-Jan-1853. Lucy is buried in the Newington Cemetery with her husband. The Welles-Robbins stone shows her as; Lucy Lowrey / Robbins / His Wife / Born June 7, 1829 / Died June 20, 1907.

Welles, Martin (21) was born in Minnesota. He was a single student who resided with his siblings and parents; Roger and Mercy D. (88, 95). He was baptized on 10-Feb-1861 in Newington. Martin died in Farmington, Connecticut on 8-Oct-1943 aged 84-5-21 and is buried in the Newington Cemetery. His headstone reads; Martin Welles / Apr. 15, 1859 / Oct. 6, 1943. There is a discrepancy, of 2 days, for the date of death between the burial permit and headstone.

Welles, Mary C. (19) was a single student who resided with her siblings and parents; Roger and Mercy D. (88, 95). Mary Crowell Welles was baptized in Newington on 4-May-1862. Mary Cromwell Welles died in Newington on 2-Jan-1930 at the age of 69-2-1. She is buried in the Newington Cemetery with other family members and her headstone reads; Mary Crowell / Welles / Nov. 1, 1860 – Jan. 2, 1930. Her burial permit lists her middle name as Cromwell but both her baptism record and headstone give it as Crowell.

Welles, Mary R. (23) was single and resided with her sister and parents; Edwin and Lucy L. (58, 64). Mary Robbins Welles was baptized on 29-Mar-1857 in Newington.

Welles, Mercy D. (47) was born in Massachusetts. She was married and resided with her children and husband; Roger Welles (88. 95). Mercy died in Newington on 17-Aug-1922 aged 89-11-17. Her headstone in the Newington Cemetery reads; Mercy Delano Aikin / Wife Of / Roger Welles / Aug. 31, 1832 – Aug. 17, 1922.

Welles, Roger (51) was a married lawyer and head of household (88, 95). His tax levy was shown as $3,660 which included: 1 house, 68 acres of land, 8 head of livestock, 1 coach, and 1 piano. The property was listed as: Old Home Lot – 18 ac, New – 11 ac, Belden – 2 ac, Mountain – 5 ac, and Whittlesey – 32 ac. He was elected as a School Visitor at the 4-Oct-1880 town meeting. Roger, son of Roger and Electa, was baptized in Newington on 12-Jul-1829 and died there on 15-May-1904 at the age of 75-2-8. His headstone in the Newington Cemetery reads; Roger Welles / Mar. 7, 1829 – May 15, 1904.

Welles, Roger Jr. (17) was in school and lived with his siblings and parents; Roger and Mercy D. (88, 95). Roger Welles Welles was baptized in Newington on 21-Jun-1863. His burial permit indicates he died in New York on 26-Apr-1932 at the age of 69. He has a table type monument in the Newington Cemetery. Also see the 18-Jun-1880 entry in the Newington Happenings section for more information on Roger.

Wells, Augusta C. (26) was a single school teacher who resided with her brother, William G. Wells (170, 178).

Wells, Chas. J. (23) was a single farmer who was head of household (119, 126). He had a tax levy valued at $2,365 which included: 1 house, 43 acres of land, and 1 head of livestock. The property was listed as: Home Lot – 30 ac and Walnut Hill – 13 ac. Charles also had a joint tax levy with Wm. G. Wells that was shown as $3,350 which included: 1 house, 38 acres of land, 18 head of livestock, and $300 money at interest. That property was known as: Home Lot – 8 ac, Dix – 10 ac, Black Oak – 12 ac, and Webster – 8 ac.

Wells, Cornelia D. (64) was a widow who resided with her son; William G. Wells (170, 178). She had a tax levy valued at $1,540 which included: 1 piano and $1,500 money at interest. Cornelia Deming, daughter of Jedediah and Mary, was baptized on 19-Aug-1821 in Newington and later married William Wells there on 3-Sep-1846. She is buried in the Newington Cemetery with her husband William. The headstone lists her as; Cornelia D. / His Wife / Died Mar. 25, 1890 / AE 74.

Wells, William G. (28) was a single farmer who was head of household (170, 178). William shared a tax levy with Wm. G. Wells that was valued at $3,350 which included: 1 house, 38 acres of land, 18 head of livestock, and $300 money at interest. The property was known as: Home Lot – 8 ac, Dix – 10 ac, Black Oak – 12 ac, and Webster – 8 ac. William Gaylord Wells, son of William and Cornelia, was baptized in Newington on 12-Sep-1852. He is buried in Fairhaven Memorial Park in Santa Ana, California, the stone reads; William G. Wells / 1852 – 1912.

West, William (15) was from Wisconsin and worked as a laborer in the household of Catherine Byrne (126, 133).

Wetherell, Allan (70) resided in the household of Edward L. Wetherell (87, 94). His relationship to the head of household and his marital status are left blank on the census record.

Wetherell, Clinton E. (9) lived with his siblings and parents; Edward L. and Sarah F. (87, 94). He died in Hartford, Connecticut on 4-May-1950 at the age of 79 and is buried in the Newington Cemetery.

Wetherell, Edward L. (32) was a married farm laborer who was head of household (87, 94). His tax levy was $270 which included: ½ of a house and 1 head of livestock. Edward was appointed as a Juror by the Town Selectmen at the 5-Jan-1880 town meeting and later elected to serve on the Board of Relief at the meeting of 4-Oct-1880. He died in West Hartford, Connecticut on 16-Mar-1928 aged 80-0-14 and is buried in the Newington Cemetery.

Wetherell, Harriet A. (38) was single and worked as a dress maker. She resided with her brother and parents; Lyman and Prudence (89, 96).

Wetherell, Hubert M. (7) lived with his siblings and parents; Edward L. and Sarah F. (87, 94). He may be buried in Glendale, California.

Wetherell, James (23) was single and worked as a farm laborer in the household of Newton Osborne (77, 84).

Wetherell, Lyman (61) was married, worked as a blacksmith, and was head of household (89, 96). His tax levy was $1,273 which included: 1 house, 24 acres of land, and 7 head of livestock. The property was described as: Home Lot – 3 ac, Mountain – 21 ac (1 acre had been abated from the original amount of 22 ac), and New – 5 ac (a note states this entire 5 ac was abated).

Wetherell, Olin L. (34) was a single stone cutter who resided with his sister and parents; Lyman and Prudence (89, 96). He is buried in the Newington Cemetery with his wife Maria. Their headstone lists him as; Olin L. Wetherell / 1845 – 1917.

Wetherell, Prudence (60) was married and resided with her children and husband Lyman Wetherell (89, 96).

Wetherell, Sarah F. (31) was from New York and married. She resided with her children and husband, Edward L. Wetherell (87, 94). Sarah Francis Wetherell died in West Hartford, Connecticut on 19-Sep-1918 at the age of 69-4-20.

Whaples, Calvin (58) was a married farmer who was head of household (133, 139). His tax levy was $657 (surcharge) which included: 1 house, 12 acres of land, and 2 head of livestock. At the 4-Oct-1880 town meeting he was elected as a Grand Juror. He appears to have died in 1914 and is buried in the Newington Cemetery.

Whaples, Chas. W. (4) was born in Maryland and lived with his siblings and father Horace Whaples (65, 72).

Whaples, David C. (28) was a single farm laborer who was head of household (65, 71). His tax levy was $220 (surcharge) which included: 1 house and 3 head of livestock. David was elected as a Hayward (Town official in charge of fences and enclosures) at the 4-Oct-1880 town meeting. He died in Newington on 21-Aug-1936 aged 85-6-30.

Whaples, Geo. N. (8) was born in Maryland and lived with his siblings and father Horace Whaples (65, 72).

Whaples, Gracie M. (10) was in school and lived with her siblings and parents, Shubael H. and Mary M. (6, 9). She is buried in the Newington Cemetery with her parents, the Whaples headstone shows her as; Grace M. Whaples / July 30, 1869 / Sept. 13, 1892.

Whaples, Horace (35) was widowed and worked as a farm laborer. He was head of household (65, 72).

Whaples, Lucy (52) was from Massachusetts and resided with her daughter and husband, Calvin Whaples (133, 139).

Whaples, Martha (68) was a widow who resided with her son, David C. Whaples (65, 71). The headstone she shares with her husband, Henry, in the Newington Cemetery lists her as; Martha Culver / His Wife / 1811 – 1907.

Whaples, Mary M. (34) was married and resided with her children and husband, Shubael Whaples (6, 9). Mary Maria Whaples died on 17-Mar-1927 in Newington, aged 81-4-21. She is buried with her husband in the Newington Cemetery. The Whaples stone lists her as; Mary M. Drew His Wife / Oct. 26, 1845 – Mar. 17, 1927.

Whaples, Minnie M. (15) was in school and lived with her sister and parents, Shubael H. and Mary M. (6, 9). She is buried in the Newington Cemetery with her parents, the Whaples headstone shows her as; Minnie M. Whaples Their Daughter / Sept. 19, 1866 – Jan. 20, 1901.

Whaples, Nancy (88) was a widow who resided in the household of her son, Calvin Whaples (133, 139). Mrs. Arden Whaples was also listed on the Supplemental Schedule for the 1880 census. She was listed in the pauper section with the disability of "old age". She appears to have died after the census in 1880 and is buried in the Newington Cemetery.

Whaples, Sarah C. (19) was single and resided with her parents, Calvin and Lucy (133, 139).

Whaples, Shubael H. (40) was a married farmer and head of household (6, 9). His tax levy was valued at $1,575 which included: 13 head of livestock, 1 piano, and $1,000 money at interest. Shubael Hart Whaples, son of Elisha and Amanda A., was baptized in Newington on 20-Sep-1840. He was elected as a Grand Juror at the 4-Oct-1880 town meeting. The Whaples headstone in the Newington Cemetery, lists him as; Shubael H. Whaples / Apr. 18, 1840 – June 5, 1899.

Whaples, un-named (5/12, 5 mos.) born in January 1880. An un-named twin boy who was born in Maryland and lived with his brothers and father, Horace (65, 72).

Whaples, un-named (5/12, 5 mos.) born in January 1880. An un-named twin boy who was born in Maryland and lived with his brothers and father, Horace (65, 72).

Wheeler, Maria (70) was a widow who worked as a house keeper in the household of Sylvester Webster (160, 168).

Whitford, Ernest R. (17) was apprenticed to a potter and lived with his siblings and parents, Loren R. and Sarah E. (36, 42).

Whitford, George M. (7) lived with his siblings and parents, Loren R. and Sarah E. (36, 42). George is buried with his mother and wife in the Saint James Cemetery in Glastonbury, Connecticut. The Whitford stone lists him as; George M. Whitford / 1871 – 1936.

Whitford, Ida M. (14) was in school and lived with her siblings and parents, Loren R. and Sarah E. (36, 42). Ida is buried with her husband, Frederick Andrews, in the Fairview Cemetery in New Britain, Connecticut. The headstone shows her as; His Wife / Ida M. Whitford / 1865 – 1954.

Whitford, Loren R. (52) was a married carpenter and head of household (36, 42).

Whitford, Sarah E. (36) was married and resided with her children and husband, Loren R. Whitford (36, 42). She is buried in the Saint James Cemetery in Glastonbury, Connecticut. The Whitford headstone shows her as; Sarah E. / Wife of Lorin R. Whitford / Feb. 15, 1845 – Apr. 24, 1902.

Whitford, William H. (12) was in school and lived with his siblings and parents, Loren R. and Sarah E. (36, 42).

Whittlesey, Cornelia (55) was born in Massachusetts, single and resided with the family of her brother Heman Whittlesey (81, 88). She was noted as being insane on the census record. Cornelia was also listed on the Supplemental Schedule for the 1880 census in the insane section with the disease of Mania. She appears to have spent a good deal of time in asylums and had been discharged in July of 1879. Her headstone in the Newington Cemetery reads; Cornelia Whittlesey / Born / May 26, 1825 / Died / Aug. 6, 1885.

Whittlesey, Georgiana (20) resided with her brother and parents, Heman and Unice (81, 88). Georgeanna Whittlesey was baptized in Newington on 22-Dec-1859.

Whittlesey, Hannah L. (59) was single and head of household (115, 122). She is buried in the Newington Cemetery and her headstone reads; Hannah L. Whittlesey / Died / Sept. 18, 1891 / Aged 72 Yrs.

Whittlesey, Heman (56) was from Massachusetts, married and worked as a farmer. He was head of household (81, 88). His tax levy was shown as $7,800 which included: 1 house, 117 1/3 acres of land, 19 head of livestock, 2 coaches, 1 piano, and $1,400 money at interest. The property was listed as: Home Lot – 73 ac, Williams – 29 ac, Green Swamp – 12 ac, Dirt Swamp – 1/3 ac, and Rear Swamp – 3 ac. Heman A. Whittlesey married Eunice C. Lattimer in Newington on 21-Jan-1847. He was appointed as a Juror by the Town Selectmen at the 5-Jan-1880 town meeting and later elected as a Justice of the Peace at the 8-Nov-1880 meeting. The Hale Collection lists his burial in the Newington Cemetery as; Heman A. Whittlesey Oct. 25, 1823 – Nov. 22, 1902.

Whittlesey, Heman C. (22) was a single student who resided with his sister and parents, Heman and Unice (81, 88). Heman Charles Whittlesey was baptized on 19-Jul-1857 in Newington. He is buried in the Indian Hill Cemetery in Middletown, Connecticut. The stone reads; Heman Charles Whittlesey / Jan. 4, 1857 / Dec. 13, 1923.

Whittlesey, Unice (53) resided with her children and husband, Heman Whittlesey (81, 88). Eunice Cordelia Lattimer, daughter of Erastus and Seviah, was baptized in Newington on 7-Oct-1827 and later married Heman Whittlesey there on 21-Jan-1847. The Hale Collection lists her burial in the Newington Cemetery as; Eunice C. Whittlesey Sept. 14, 1825 – May 22, 1910.

Wickham, Esther L. (12) was in school and lived with the family of her uncle, Wm. E. Potter (33, 39).

Wirt, James H. (53) was from Massachusetts, married, and worked as a building mover. He was also head of household (86, 93).

Wirt, Mary E. (33) was from England and resided with her husband, James H. Wirt (86, 93). At the time of the census she was suffering from a malaria fever.

Woodward, Alfred J. (10 mos.) was born in Nov. 1879 and lived with his siblings and parents, J. Everett and Percy E. (48, 54).

Woodward, Benj. P. (4) lived with his siblings and parents, J. Everett and Percy E. (48, 54). He is buried with his wife in the Spring Grove Cemetery in Hartford, Connecticut. The Woodward stone shows him as; Benjamin Woodward / 1876 – 1947.

Woodward, Frederick E. (14) lived with his siblings and parents, J. Everett and Percy E. (48, 54).

Woodward, J. Everett (42) was a married painter and head of household (48, 54). The Hale Collection lists his burial in the Spring Grove Cemetery in Hartford, Connecticut as; J. Everett Woodward 1837 – 1894.

Woodward, Percy E. (40) was married and resided with her children and husband, J. Everett Woodward (48, 54). The Hale Collection lists her in the Spring Grove Cemetery in Hartford, Connecticut as; Percy E.R. Woodward wife of J. Everett 1837 – 1894.

Woodward, Wm. S. (10) lived with his siblings and parents, J. Everett and Percy E. (48, 54).

_____, Louis (23) was from Sweden, single, and worked as a farm laborer in the household of Willis P. Davis (71, 78). Under the surname section on the census the notation "not able to tell" is listed. He is also noted as unable to read or write.

_____, Nelson (30) was from Sweden, single, and worked as a farm laborer in the household of Willis P. Davis (71, 78). Under the surname section on the census the notation "not able to tell" is listed. He is also noted as unable to read or write.

Adams, Chauncey was noted as a Wethersfield, Connecticut resident. His Newington tax levy was listed as $97 for 6 ½ acres of land. Chauncey (71) worked as a farmer, was a widower, and lived with family members in Wethersfield. He is buried in the Wethersfield Village Cemetery. His headstone reads; Chauncey Adams / Died / June 27, 1883 / AE 75.

Allen, Abel was listed as a resident of Wethersfield, Connecticut. His Newington tax levy was shown as $700 for 28 acres of land. Abel (60) was a farmer who lived in Wethersfield with his family.

Belden, E.S. was shown as a resident of Rocky Hill, Connecticut. E.S. and S. Belden had a joint tax levy in Newington listed as $675 for 27 acres of land. There are a number of different Belden families in Rocky Hill on the census, I could not definitively identify this individual.

Belden, S. was shown as a resident of Rocky Hill, Connecticut. S. and E.S. Belden had a joint tax levy in Newington listed as $675 for 27 acres of land. There are a number of different Belden families in Rocky Hill on the census, I could not definitively identify this individual.

Billings, Nathaniel was listed as a resident of Wethersfield, Connecticut. His Newington tax levy was valued at $67 for 6 ¾ acres of land. Nathaniel (66) was a farmer from Massachusetts. He lived with his family in Wethersfield. The Billings headstone in the Wethersfield Village Cemetery lists him as; Nathaniel Billings with no dates.

Booth, Wm. S. was noted as a resident of New Britain, Connecticut. His Newington tax levy was listed as $900 for 30 acres of land. William (54) lived on East Main Street in New Britain with his family (his occupation is illegible). His headstone in the Fairview Cemetery in New Britain reads; William S. Booth / Died / Sept. 25, 1888 / Aged 62 Y'rs.

Brewer, Sarah Mrs. was listed as a resident of Hartford, Connecticut. Her Newington tax levy was shown as $100 for 2 acres of land. Mrs. Brewer could not be located in Hartford on the 1880 census record.

Brinley, George was listed as a resident of Hartford, Connecticut. His Newington tax levy was shown as $75 for 1 acre of land. George (38) was a farmer who resided with his family on Blue Hills Street in Hartford. He is buried in the Old North Cemetery in Hartford, the headstone lists him as; George Brinley / Born Apr. 10, 1842 / Died Aug. 24, 1892.

Bronson, Nathan S. was listed as a New Britain, Connecticut resident. His Newington tax levy was shown as $600 for 20 acres of land. Nathan (42) was a farmer who lived with his family in New Britain. His headstone in the Fairview Cemetery in New Britain reads; Nathan S. Bronson / Nov. 20, 1837 – May 1, 1911.

Butler, Ashbel was shown as a resident of Wethersfield, Connecticut. His Newington tax levy was listed as $80 for 4 acres of land. Mr. Butler could not be located in Wethersfield on the census record.

Butler, Hez. was listed as a resident of Wethersfield, Connecticut. His Newington tax levy is shown as $160 for 4 acres of land. Hezekiah (47) was an unmarried farmer who lived with family members in

Wethersfield. He appears to be buried in the Cedar Hill Cemetery in Hartford, Connecticut. He is listed on headstone there as; Hezekiah Butler / 1833 – 1906.

Butler, Jared Estate was listed as a resident of Wethersfield, Connecticut. The Newington tax levy for Mr. Butler was shown as $60 for 3 acres of land. Jared (61) was an unmarried carpenter who resided in Wethersfield. He died prior to the certification of the Newington tax levy that is why it is listed in the name of his estate. Jared is buried in the Cedar Hill Cemetery in Hartford, Connecticut. The monument lists him as; Jared J. Butler / Born Aug. 20, 1818 / Died Oct. 31, 1880.

Cadwell, Amasa was noted as a resident of Wethersfield, Connecticut. His Newington tax levy was $140 for 3 ½ acres of land. Amasa (72) was a farmer who lived with his family in Wethersfield. He is buried in the Cedar Hill Cemetery in Hartford, Connecticut. His headstone reads; Amasa Cadwell / July 31, 1809 / Feb. 19, 1895.

Chambers, Francis was shown as a resident of New Britain, Connecticut. The Newington tax levy for Francis was listed as $100 for 4 acres of land. This person could not be located in New Britain on the census record.

Churchill, Simeon Heirs were noted as residents of Wethersfield, Connecticut. The Newington levy was listed as $210 for 6 acres of land. There are a number of Churchill families in Wethersfield on the census record that this could apply to.

Churchill, Stephen B. Estate was listed as a resident of Wethersfield, Connecticut. The Newington tax levy for the estate was noted as $420 for 12 acres of land. Stephen had died in 1879 and is buried in Wethersfield Village Cemetery. His headstone reads; Stephen B. Churchill / Died / Dec. 2, 1879 / AE 49. His widow Amelia resided in Wethersfield with their children on the census record.

Clark, Edward L. Mrs. was listed as a New Britain, Connecticut resident. Her Newington tax levy was shown as $217 for 7 ¼ acres of land. This person could not be located in New Britain in the census record.

Clark, Sylvester was shown as a resident of Wethersfield, Connecticut. His Newington tax levy was listed as $200 for 10 acres of land. Sylvester (72) worked as a farm laborer and resided with his family in Wethersfield.

Coleman, Alfred Heirs were listed as residents of Wethersfield, Connecticut. Their Newington tax levy was noted as $15 for 1 acre of land. There are a number of Coleman individuals in Wethersfield who could be these heirs.

Coleman, Roswell was noted as a Wethersfield, Connecticut resident. His Newington tax levy was valued at $825 for 27 ½ acres of land. Roswell (56) was a farmer who lived in Wethersfield with his family. He is buried in the Wethersfield Village Cemetery. The monument lists him as; Roswell Coleman / 1821 – 1895.

Cone, Joseph H. was listed as a resident of Hartford, Connecticut. Joseph H. and Wm. E. Cone had a joint tax levy in Newington shown as $180 for 3 acres of land. Joseph (45) worked as a hardware dealer and lived with his family on Asylum Avenue in Hartford. A monument in the Cedar Hill Cemetery in Hartford shows him as; Joseph H. Cone / Feb. 5, 1836 / July 7, 1892.

Cone, Wm. E. was shown as a resident of Hartford, Connecticut. Wm. E. and Joseph H. Cone had a joint tax levy in Newington shown as $180 for 3 acres of land. Wm. (37) worked as a merchant and lived as a boarder in a house on Main Street in Hartford. The Cone monument in the North Cemetery in West Hartford, Connecticut shows him as; William Ezra Cone / Born June 14, 1842 / Died Oct. 1, 1925.

Curtis, Hapey C. was listed as a Wethersfield, Connecticut resident. Her Newington tax levy was valued at $300 for 10 acres of land. Hapey Curtiss (74) was a widow who lived with her son in Wethersfield.

Curtiss, H.B. Mrs. was listed as a resident of Wethersfield, Connecticut. Her Newington tax levy was noted as $160 for 4 acres of land. I could not locate anyone with this name in Wethersfield on the census record.

Day, Asa W. was shown as a resident of Hartford, Connecticut. The Newington tax levy for Asa was shown as $60 for 1 acre of land. Asa (36) worked in real estate. He lived with his family on Willard Street in Hartford. Asa is buried in the Bellefontaine Cemetery in St. Louis, Missouri. The stone there lists him as; Asa W. Day / Born / Marlborough Conn. / 1844 – 1913.

Dillings, Eliza K. was listed as a resident of Wethersfield, Connecticut. Her Newington tax levy was noted as $490 for 28 acres of land. Eliza (38) resided with her husband in Wethersfield. She is buried in the Wethersfield Village Cemetery. The Dillings monument lists her as; Eliza K. His Wife / Died June 2, 1904 / Aged 64.

Dix, Roswell N. was shown as a resident of Wethersfield, Connecticut. He had two separate Newington tax levies listed as $120 for 8 acres of land and $35 for 3 ½ acres of land. Roswell (45) was a farmer who lived with his family in Wethersfield. He is buried in Cedar Hill Cemetery in Hartford, Connecticut. His headstone reads; Roswell Newton Dix / 1835 – 1899.

Dowdell, Michael was shown as a resident of Berlin, Connecticut. His Newington tax levy was $375 for 15 acres of land. Michael (38) was from Ireland and worked in a factory. He lived with his family in Berlin.

Dwight, Henry C. Mrs. [Sarah] was listed as a Hartford, Connecticut resident. A Newington tax levy existed for Mrs. Henry C. Dwight in the amount of $30 for 2 ½ acres of land. Sarah (58) was a widow who lived as a boarder on Bellevue Street in Hartford. Henry had died in 1875 and Sarah is the only individual with the Dwight surname in Hartford on the 1880 census.

Ellsworth, Pinkney W. was shown as a resident of Hartford, Connecticut. His Newington tax levy was listed as $1,400 for 2 houses. Pinkney (65) was a married physician and surgeon who lived on Collins Street, with his family, in Hartford. He died in 1896 and is buried in the Old North Cemetery in Hartford.

Flagg, Chas. N. was shown as resident of Hartford, Connecticut. His Newington tax levy was $60 for 1/8 of an acre of land. He could not be located in Hartford on the 1880 census record.

Francis, Maria was listed as a resident of Wethersfield, Connecticut. Her Newington tax levy was shown as $20 for 1 acre of land. She could not be located on the census record in Wethersfield.

Gillagan, John was shown as a resident of Berlin, Connecticut. His Newington tax levy was originally valued at $440 for 20 acres of land. Those totals were crossed through and changed to 14 ½ acres of land valued at $22 an acre (no new total was listed). John Gilligan (42) was a farmer from Ireland and lived with his family in Berlin.

Goodrich, Elizur was listed as a resident of Wethersfield, Connecticut. His Newington tax levy was shown as $60 for 2 acres of land. Mr. Goodrich could not be located in Wethersfield on the census record.

Griswold, Chas. R. was listed as a resident of Cromwell, Connecticut. His Newington tax levy was valued at $100 for 4 acres of land. This individual could not be located in Cromwell on the census record.

Griswold, Jacob Mrs. was listed as a resident of Wethersfield, Connecticut. Her Newington tax levy was valued at $40 for 5 acres of land. There are a number of Griswold individuals in Wethersfield who could be this person.

Griswold, James S. was noted as a resident of Wethersfield, Connecticut. His Newington tax levy was listed as $150 for 5 acres of land. James (65) was a farmer and member of the legislature. He lived with his family in Wethersfield. James is buried in the Wethersfield Village Cemetery. The Griswold monument lists him as; Jas. S. Griswold / 1815 – 1906.

Goodrich, Joshua Heirs were listed as residents of Wethersfield, Connecticut. The Newington tax levy for the heirs was valued at $60 for 2 acres of land. There are a number of Griswold individuals in Wethersfield who could be these heirs.

Griswold, Thos. Heirs were listed as Wethersfield, Connecticut residents. That Newington tax levy was valued at $30 for 3 acres of land. There are a number of Griswold individuals in Wethersfield who could be these heirs.

Griswold, Wells J. was shown as a Wethersfield, Connecticut resident. His Newington tax levy was listed as $100 for 4 acres of land. J. Wells (56) was a farmer who lived with his family in Wethersfield.

Hamner, John was listed as a resident of Wethersfield, Connecticut. His Newington tax levy was shown as $210 for 6 acres of land. John (79) was a farmer who resided with his family in Wethersfield.

Hoye, Michael was listed as a resident of West Hartford, Connecticut. His Newington tax levy was $240 for 6 acres of land. Michael (46) was from Ireland and worked as a farmer. He resided with his family in West Hartford. He appears to have died in 1913 and is buried in the Saint Mary Cemetery in New Britain, Connecticut.

Johnson, Andrew had no residence listed. His tax levy for 1 house was $600.

Johnson, Elisha was another Hartford, Connecticut resident. His Newington tax levy was valued at $980 for 1 house and 16 acres of land. Elisha (62) was a married lawyer who lived with his family on Garden Street in Hartford. He is buried, with his wife, in the Spring Grove Cemetery in Hartford. The monument shows him as; Elisha Johnson / May 1, 1818 / Feb. 18, 1891.

Kellogg, Chas E. was listed as a resident of West Hartford, Connecticut. The Newington tax levy for him was $504 for 14 acres of land. Charles (40) lived with his family in West Hartford (his occupation on the census is illegible). His headstone in the Cedar Hill Cemetery in Hartford, Connecticut reads; Charles E. Kellogg / Dec. 5, 1839 / Aug. 27, 1933.

Kelly, Thomas Mrs. was noted as a resident in Rocky Hill, Connecticut. Her Newington tax levy was $120 for 6 acres of land. No one by this name was located in Rocky Hill on the census record. It's possible that it could be Sarah Kelley who was a widow living in Rocky Hill in 1880.

Kelsey, David is noted as a resident of New Britain, Connecticut. However, he had no assessment attached to his name.

Moore, James P. was shown as a New Britain, Connecticut resident. His Newington tax levy was valued at $390 for 13 acres of land. James (61) worked as a farmer and resided with his family on Hart Street in New Britain. His headstone in the Fairview Cemetery in New Britain reads; James P. Moore / Born Jany. 24, 1819 / Died Mar. 4, 1903.

Morris, John E. was shown as a Hartford, Connecticut resident. His Newington tax levy was $120 for 2 acres of land. John (36) was born in Massachusetts and worked as an insurance officer. He lived in Hartford on Ward Street with his family. His headstone in the Cedar Hill Cemetery in Hartford lists him as; John Emery Morris / November 30, 1843 / May 30, 1911.

Norton, Ruth S. had no residence listed. Her tax levy for 9 acres of land and 1 house was shown as $1360. Ruth (47) was a widow living with her children in Winchester, Connecticut.

Pease, Julius H. was noted as a resident of New Britain, Connecticut. His Newington tax levy was listed as $82 for 2 ¾ acres of land. Julius (66) worked as a farmer and lived with his family in New Britain. He is buried in the Fairview Cemetery in New Britain. The headstone reads; Julius W. Pease / Colebrook, CT 1814 / New Britain, CT 1908.

Purinton, Joseph D. was noted as a resident of Nebraska. His Newington tax levy was valued at $4,540 which included 1 house and 74 acres of land. The property was listed as: Home Lot 6 ac, East Side 10 ac, Second 10 ac, Third 15 ac, Fourth 15 ac, and Fifth 18 ac. He could not be located in Nebraska on the census record. He seems to have died in 1932 and is buried in Seattle, Washington.

Rand, George D. was listed as a resident of Boston, Massachusetts. His Newington tax levy for 1 acre of land was $60. George H. Rand (48) was a grocer from Massachusetts. He lived with his family on Hancock Street in Boston. This may be the same person.

Redfield, Edward was shown as a resident of Essex, Connecticut. His Newington tax levy for 9 acres of land was $270. Edward (54) was a treasurer for a bank and resided with his family in Essex. He is buried in the Prospect Hill Cemetery in Essex. His headstone reads; In Memory Of / Edward W. Redfield / Who Died / Aug. 9th 1898 / In The 73rd Year / Of His Age.

Reynolds, John was listed as a Farmington, Connecticut resident. His Newington tax levy was shown as $352 for 7 acres of land and 1 building. This individual could not be located in Farmington on the census record.

Rhodes, Chauncey was listed as a resident of Hartford, Connecticut. There was a joint tax levy in Newington for C. and H.B. Rhodes that totaled $560 for 28 acres of land. Chauncey (63) was a retired merchant who lived with his family in Hartford. He is listed on a Rhodes monument in the Cedar Hill Cemetery in Hartford as; Chauncey Rhodes / Born Jan. 10, 1815 / Died Feb. 6, 1901.

Rhodes, Henry B. was shown as a Hartford, Connecticut resident. There was a joint tax levy in Newington for H.B. and C. Rhodes that totaled $560 for 28 acres of land. Henry (61) was a retired merchant who resided with his family on Hudson Street in Hartford. The Rhodes monument in the Cedar Hill Cemetery in Hartford lists him as; Henry B. Rhodes / Born Jan. 8, 1819 – Died Mar. 6, 1886.

Robbins, Sarah was listed as a resident of Rocky Hill, Connecticut. Her original Newington tax levy was valued at $928 for 29 acres of land which was later reduced to $140 for 7 acres of land. A note indicates "22 acres taken off by Board of relief". Sarah F. (50) lived with her husband, Jason A., in Rocky Hill. She is buried with her husband in the Center Cemetery in Rocky Hill. The Robbins monument shows her as; Sarah His Wife / Died Nov. 12, 1890 / Aged 61 Yrs.

Robbins, Wm. Heirs were listed as residents of Wethersfield, Connecticut. Their Newington tax levy was shown as $48 for 8 acres of land. There are a number Robbins individuals residing in Wethersfield who could be these heirs.

Rowley, David E. was listed as a Berlin, Connecticut resident. His Newington tax levy was shown as $540 for 18 acres of land. David (52) worked as a farmer and lived with his family in Berlin. His headstone in the Church Street Cemetery in Newington lists him as; David E. Rowley / Born Mar. 30, 1828 / Died Aug. 8, 1892.

Russell, Gurdon W. was listed as a resident of Hartford, Connecticut. His Newington tax levy was listed as $3,150 for 1 house and 86 acres of land. Gurdon (65) was a married physician who lived with his family on Main Street in Hartford. He is buried with his wife, Sarah, in the Cedar Hill Cemetery in Hartford. The monument lists him as; Gurdon Wadsworth Russell / Born Apr. 10, 1815 – Died Feb. 3, 1909.

Seymour, Michael L. was listed as a Hartford, Connecticut resident. His Newington tax levy was valued at $120 for 2 acres of land. Michael (54) was shown as M.L. Seymour on the census record. He was a farmer who lived with his family on New Britain Avenue in Hartford. Michael is buried with family members in the Cedar Hill Cemetery in Hartford. The headstone lists him as; Michael Lemuel Seymour / 1826 – 1897.

Seymour, Sylvester was shown as a resident of Hartford, Connecticut. His Newington tax levy was valued at $420 for 7 acres of land. Sylvester (62) was a farmer who resided with his family on New Britain Avenue in Hartford. His headstone in the Cedar Hill Cemetery in Hartford lists him as; Sylvester Seymour / 1818 – 1890.

Seymour, Woster B. was listed as a resident of Hartford, Connecticut. His Newington tax levy was listed as $600 for 17 ½ acres of land. Wooster (60) was a farmer who lived with his family on New Britain Avenue in Hartford. His headstone in the Cedar Hill Cemetery in Hartford lists him as; Wooster B. Seymour / 1820 – 1888.

Shepard, Edward Heirs were listed as Wethersfield, Connecticut residents. Their Newington tax levy was shown as $90 for 6 acres of land. Edward appears to have died in 1862. Two of his surviving daughters, Mary and Elizabeth, were living in Wethersfield in 1880.

Standish, Ira was noted as a resident of Wethersfield, Connecticut. His Newington tax levy was valued at $150 for 3 acres of land. Ira (47) was a farmer who lived with his family in Wethersfield. He is buried in the Cedar Hill Cemetery in Hartford, Connecticut. The stone there reads; Ira Myles Standish / Jul. 5, 1832 – Dec. 30, 1895.

Steele, Betsey was listed as a Berlin, Connecticut resident. Her Newington tax levy was shown as $30 for 2 ½ acres of land. Betsey (73) was single and lived with her nephew, Samuel Talmadge, in Berlin.

Steele, Maria was shown as a resident of Berlin, Connecticut. She had a Newington tax levy valued at $12 for 1 ½ acres of land. Maria (71) was single and resided with her nephew, Samuel Talmadge, in Berlin.

Stephens, Alexander was listed as a resident of Rocky Hill, Connecticut. His Newington tax levy was shown as $270 for 18 acres of land. Alexander Stevens (65) was a farmer living with his family in Rocky Hill. He is buried in the Beckley Cemetery in Berlin, Connecticut. The headstone lists him as; Alexander Stevens / Died Feb. 11, 1896 / AE 81.

Swift, Thomas was a listed as a Hartford, Connecticut resident. His Newington tax levy was $120 for 2 acres of land. Thomas (45) was from England and worked as a gold beater. He lived with his family on Judson Street in Hartford.

Talmadge, Samuel F. was shown as a resident of Berlin, Connecticut. His Newington tax levy was for $5 for 1 acre of land. Samuel (37) was single and worked as a farmer in Berlin.

Terry, Clarence was listed as a Hartford, Connecticut resident. His Newington tax levy was $90 for 1 ½ acres of land. Clarence (39) worked as a clerk and lived with his family on Sumner Street in Hartford. He is buried in the Spring Grove Cemetery in Hartford. The monument lists him as; Clarence Terry / Mar. 19, 1841 – May 18, 1886.

Vibberts, Lester A. was noted as a resident of New Britain, Connecticut. His Newington tax levy was listed as $2,356 for 76 acres of land. Lester (50) worked as a farmer and resided with his family in New Britain. He is buried in the Fairview Cemetery in New Britain and his headstone reads; Lester A. Vibberts / Oct. 15, 1829 – July 31, 1908.

Ward, Frederick W. was listed as a Middletown, Connecticut resident. His Newington tax levy for 6 acres of land was valued at $100. Frederick (44) worked as a livery and lived with his family in the West Long Hill District of Middletown.

Webster, Luther S. was shown as a resident of Berlin, Connecticut. His Newington tax levy was shown as $527 for 17 acres of land. Luther (54) worked as a farmer and resided with his family in Berlin. He appears to have died in 1908 and is buried in the Maple Cemetery in Berlin.

Welles, Leonard R. was listed as a Wethersfield, Connecticut resident. His Newington tax levy was noted as $50 for 2 acres of land. Leonard (76) was a farmer who lived in Wethersfield with his wife. He is buried in the Cedar Hill Cemetery in Hartford, Connecticut. The headstone shows him as; Leonard R. Welles / Died May 5, 1883 / Aged 80 Years.

Wells, Ashbel Heirs were noted as Wethersfield, Connecticut residents. Their Newington tax levy was valued at $175 for 7 acres of land. Ashbel seems to have died in 1872. No definitive information was located about these heirs in Wethersfield.

Wells, George was listed as a resident of Iowa. His tax levy in Newington was shown as $4,240 which included: 1 house, 113 acres of land, and 11 head of livestock. The property was listed as: Home Lot – 27 ac, West – 10 ac, Middle – 27 ac, South – 15 ac, Belden – 30 ac, and Welles – 4 ac. George (59) was a married farmer who lived in Shiloh, Grundy County, Iowa. He is buried in the Rose Hill Cemetery in Grundy, Iowa with his wife, Sarah and son Frank. The monument there lists him as: George Wells / Born May 14, 1821 / Died Aug. 2, 1906.

Wells, Levi S. was listed as a New Britain, Connecticut resident. His Newington tax levy was shown as $1,120 for 35 acres of land. Levi (55) worked as a farmer and lived with his family in New Britain. He is buried in the Fairview Cemetery in New Britain. The headstone lists him as; Levi Sedgwick Wells / Died / Dec. 12, 1904 / Aged 79 Y'rs.

Wells, Nancy was shown as a Wethersfield, Connecticut resident. Her Newington tax levy was for $644 for 28 acres of land. Nancy Welles (77) was single and resided in Wethersfield. She is buried in the Wethersfield Village Cemetery and her headstone reads; In Memory Of / Nancy Wells / Who Died June 27, 1889 / Aged 87 Years.

Wells, Samuel R. was noted as a resident of Wethersfield, Connecticut. His Newington tax levy was shown as $60 for 3 acres of land. Mr. Wells could not be located in Wethersfield on the census record. He does appear to have died in 1888 and is buried in the Wethersfield Village Cemetery.

Willard, Daniel H. was listed as a resident of Hartford, Connecticut. His tax levy in Newington was valued at $7,896 and included: 3 houses, 190 acres of land, and 20 head of livestock. Daniel was not located in Hartford on the 1880 census.

Willard, Wm. Heirs were listed as residents of Wethersfield, Connecticut. Their tax levy was shown as $96 for 6 acres of land. William had died in 1870. His widow, Jane G. Willard, resided in Wethersfield in 1880.

Winship, Chauncey was shown as a resident of Hartford, Connecticut. His Newington tax levy was $250 for 10 acres of land. Chauncey (67) was a farmer who lived with his family on Wethersfield Avenue in Hartford. He died in 1897 and is buried in the Cedar Hill Cemetery in Hartford.

Woodhouse, Samuel was listed as a Wethersfield, Connecticut resident. His Newington tax levy was valued at $45 for 3 acres of land. Samuel (63) was a farmer who lived in Wethersfield with his family. His monument in the Wethersfield Village Cemetery reads; Samuel Woodhouse / 1815 – 1885.

Wright, Henry B. was shown as a resident of Wethersfield, Connecticut. His Newington tax levy for 35 acres of land was valued at $630. A hand written note by his name in the levy book reads "also for orchard". Henry (47) was a farmer who lived with his wife in Wethersfield. His headstone in the Cedar Hill Cemetery in Hartford, Connecticut reds; Henry B. Wright / 1829 – 1905.

No.	Description of Property	Value
178 ½	Dwelling Houses	138,785
7158 5/8	Acres of Land	203,770
1	Stores	200
2	Mills, Manufactories	1,900
177	Horses, Asses and Mules	8,200
814	Neat Cattle	19,840
62	Sheep	124
	Swine, exceeding in value $50	145
32	Coaches, Carriages and Pleasure Wagons	2,090
	Farming Utensils exceeding in value $200	100
19	Clocks, Watches, Time Pieces and Jewelry	810
	Libraries, exceeding in value $200	2,555
26	Piano Fortes and other Musical Instruments, not exempt	45,828
	Insurance Stock	9,665
	Investments in Mechanical and Manufacturing operations	4,000
	Money at Interest in this State and elsewhere	40,038
	Money on hand, exceeding $100	6,251
	Ten Percent added for unsworn lists	6,454
		491,025
	107 Polls	
	10 Polls Abated	
	Abated for Indebtedness	4,795
		486,230

The levy was certified by the Assessors, **Chas. E. Chapman** and **Henry S. Kellogg** they swore an oath on December 15, 1880 in front of Justice of the Peace **John S. Kirkham**.

Newington Happenings 1880

All these items appeared in the *Hartford Daily Courant* during 1880. The date, page number, and title of article are noted.

9 Jan 1880 – pg. 2 – "Hartford and Vicinity: City Briefs"
The Hartford County Agricultural Society elected; **John S. Kirkham**, of Newington, as Vice-President and **S.M. Wells**, of Newington, as Recording Secretary

10 Jan 1880 – pg. 4 – "News of the State: Newington"
"Unless it is very stormy there will be another temperance meeting held at Newington Junction Sunday evening at 7 o'clock"

15 Jan 1880 – pg. 2 – "A Pleasant Occasion"
"Fish's hall, at Newington Junction, was filled Tuesday evening by friends of Mr. **William E. Potter**, a resident of the village, who has just recovered from a severe illness" Music was furnished by the "Newington String Band" led by **N. Osborn**. **M.L. Stoddard** served as prompter [caller] for the dancing after the supper. Later **J.C. Sternberg** made a speech and presented Mr. Potter with a cane from Captain C.H. Case jeweler, Asylum St in Hartford, the head of which was inscribed "Presented to Wm. E. Potter by his friends, Newington, Jany. 1880"

21 Jan 1880 – pg. 2 – "Hartford and Vicinity: City Briefs"
The funeral of **John G. Wells** (former book publisher) "will be attended from the House of **William G. Wells** at Newington, this afternoon at 1 o'clock"

27 Jan 1880 – pg. 4 – "News of the State: Newington"
"The Congregational Church has just received a nice toned bell from Jones & Co. of Troy"

5 Feb 1880 – pg. 1 – "Classified Ads: Farms for Sale" [this ad appeared 10 times in February and March]
"In Newington Junction, a farm containing about 45 acres; land in a high state of cultivation, with dwelling house, barn, and tobacco shed all in good condition. Located about one-quarter of a mile from Newington Station on N.Y. N.H. and H. railroad" Inquire The Farmers Mechanics National Bank of Hartford.

17 Mar 1880 – pg. 2 – "Killed by Cars"
An unidentified man was killed on Monday evening on the tracks near the Berlin town line. The inquest returned a verdict of "accidental death".

23 Mar 1880 – pg. 1 –"Hartford and Vicinity: City Briefs"
"Mr. **Martin Robbins**, aged 84, a leading citizen of Newington, died yesterday"

1 Apr 1880 – pg. 4 – "News of the State: Newington"
Newington Republican delegates; **M.L. Stoddard** and **J.C. Sternberg** voted as to the "Presidential question"

18 Jun 1880 – pg. 2 – "Hartford and Vicinity: City Briefs"
"**Roger Welles Jr.**, of Newington, on recommendation of General Hawley, has been selected for examination for admission to the United States Naval Academy at Annapolis"

5 Jul 1880 – pg. 2 – "Hartford and Vicinity: City Briefs"
"**Neil Murphy, Joseph Thrall** and **Albert Montly** [probably Albert Muttley], residents of Newington, will be tried in the police court this morning for creating a disturbance on a train on the Consolidated road Saturday afternoon"

12 Jul 1880 – pg. 2 – "Saturday's Storm: A Heavy Electric Shock and its Result"
As temperatures settled in the 100-106 degree range a thunder storm struck the Hartford area with the following result. "The metal parts of a harness of a horse hitched in Asylum street were bright with electric light, and a Newington team, owned by a **Mr. Gilbert**, ran away from Pearl street; the wagon was badly smashed"

4 Aug 1880 – pg. 4 – "News of the State: Republican Delegates"
Newington Delegates – State: **Frank Corbin, Jonathan Starr**; Congressional: **Roger Welles, John T. Stoddard**; Sherriff: **John R. Stoddard, Elias M. Steele**; Probate: **James Baxter, Louis A. Tracy**.

19 Aug 1880 – pg. 2 – "Real Estate Transactions"
"The Paper Mill property at Newington, known as Rockwell Mill, [sold] to parties in Manchester, terms private" [see deed dated 30-Sep-1880 in vol. 1 pg. 407]

17 Sep 1880 – pg. 2 – "Classified: Lost"
"Lost-Thursday afternoon, between this city [Hartford] and Newington, six SILVER SPOONS. The finder will be suitably rewarded by leaving the same with **J.G. Stoddard**, Newington, Conn."

23 Sep 1880 – pg. 2 – "Obituaries"
"**STODDARD** – in Newington, Sept. 20, **Lewis Allen**, son of **Carrie and Lewis Stoddard**, aged 2 years and 4 months. Funeral this (Thursday) afternoon at 2 ½ o'clock from the residence of the parents. Friends are invited to attend without further notice."

5 Oct 1880 – pg. 2 – "State Politics: Newington"
"The Republicans of the Town opened the campaign [1880 presidential campaign] with a flag-raising in front of Mr. **J.D. Seymour's** residence on Saturday evening which was the most enthusiastic political meeting held here for years" . . . "after rousing cheers for Garfield and Arthur and the state ticket, all partook of a bountiful collation which was furnished by the ladies and served on the lawn in front of Mr. **J.C. Sternberg's** residence"

4 Nov 1880 – pg. 3 – "Election Notes"
"The little town of Newington, usually democratic, sends a republican representative this year"

30 Nov 1880 – pg. 4 – "News of the State: Newington"
A horse owned by **J. Belden** took fright and "after running a short distance bringing up with a broken leg though he had not fallen down or come in contact with any object" **Dr. Creasy** determined that surgery was useless and the horse was destroyed.

18 Dec 1880 – pg. 1 – "News of the State: Newington"
"Arba Lankton's total abstinence and anti-tobacco society will hold a meeting at Newington town hall Sunday evening at 7 o'clock"

Newington Deeds 1880

The date shown for the following deeds was the date the deed was filed in the Town Clerk's office. This is not a comprehensive list of deeds from 1880 just a sampling.

16-Jan-1880 – **John H. Fish** sold 1.5 acres of land to **Emily W. Griswold** for $700. The warranty deed is recorded in volume 1 page 382 of the Newington land records.

19-Feb-1880 – **Martin Luther Jr.** and his wife **Louise** sold 2 acres of land to **Julius W. Pease**. For $825. The warranty deed is recorded in volume 1 page 383 of the Newington land records.

28-Feb-1880 – **Lester and Sophia Luce** sold two parcels of land containing 20 acres of land to **Joshua C. Luce** for $2,000. This deed was originally dated 27-Aug-1859 and likely recorded on the Wethersfield land records when Newington was still part of that town. The warranty deed is recorded in volume 1 page 384 of the Newington land records.

28-Feb-1880 – **Lester Luce** sold 50 acres of land to **Joshua C. Luce** for $2,000. This deed was originally dated 28-Aug-1876 and likely recorded on the Wethersfield land records when Newington was still part of that town. The warranty deed is recorded in volume 1 page 385 of the Newington land records.

8-Mar-1880 – **Philo F.** and his wife **Mary W. Judd** sold 10 acres of land to **William S. Booth** [a portion of that property was in New Britain] for $1,600. The warranty deed is recorded in volume 1 page 388 of the Newington land records.

29-Mar-1880 – **Abel Allen** sold 6 acres and 21 rods [21 rods equals 0.13 acres] of land to **Gurden W. Russell** for $10. The property was located on Cedar Mountain and likely was a "wood lot". This quit claim deed is filed in volume 1 page 389 of the Newington land records.

29-Mar-1880 – **Susan P. Richards** sold 6 acres of land to **William M. Richards** for $100. This deed was originally dated on 22-May-1871. The quit claim deed is filed in volume 1 page 391 of the Newington land records.

29-Mar-1880 – **Elias M. Steele**, as conservator of the **Susan P. Clark** estate, sold 26 acres of land to **William M. Richards** for $800. The warranty deed is recorded in volume 1 page 392 of the Newington land records.

13-Apr-1880 – **Charles Higgins** sold two parcels totaling 45 acres and 15 rods [45.09 acres] to **Charles J. Wells** for $2,500. That warranty deed is recorded in volume 1 page 404 of the Newington land records.

26-Apr-1880 – **Sylvester Webster** sold 11 acres of land to **Elisabeth Doherwent** for $1,200. That warranty deed is recorded in volume 1 page 394 of the Newington land records.

20-May-1880 – **Martin and Lydia A. Ellis** (husband and wife) sold 10 acres of land to **John Webster** for $1. That quit claim deed is filed in volume 1 page 396 of the Newington land records.

3-Jun-1880 – **Polly A. Shurtleff** sold 50 rods of land [0.31 acres] to **Mary Quinn** for $1,000. That warranty deed is recorded volume 1 page 399 of the Newington land records. A corrective deed was filed to add the name **Carmi Shurtleff**, husband of Polly. That corrected deed is recorded in volume 1 page 402 of the Newington land records.

16-Jun-1880 – **Martin and Lydia A. Ellis** sold a parcel of property known as the "vexation lot" [no acreage listed] to **Oliver Richards** for $150. That quit claim deed is originally dated 22-Feb-1871 and is filed in volume 2 page 208 of the Newington land records.

30-Sep-1880 – **Elvey A. Hart** sold a parcel of land formerly known as "Rockdale Mills" to **William F. Pickles** for $1,500. There was no acreage listed for this parcel on the deed. That warranty deed is recorded in volume 1 page 407 of the Newington land records.

9-Dec-1880 – **Frederick W.S. Ward** and his wife **Mary L.** sold two parcels of land totaling 5 acres to **Aholiab Corbin** for $50. The warranty deed is filed in volume 1 page 409 of the Newington land records.

13-Dec-1880 – **Lester Luce** sold 15 acres of land to **Joshua C. Luce** for $7. This deed was originally dated 24-Aug-1868 and likely had been recorded in the Wethersfield land records when Newington was still part of that town. The quit claim deed is filed in volume 1 page 412 of the Newington land records.

13-Dec-1880 – **Susan P. Richards** sold two parcels of land totaling 26 acres to **Joshua C. Luce** for $1,350. That warranty deed is filed in volume 1 page 413 of the Newington land records.

13-Dec-1880 – **Henry M. Whiting** sold 6 acres of land to **Joshua C. Luce** for $850. The warranty deed was originally dated 22-Jul-1873 and is filed in volume 1 page 414 of the Newington land records.

31-Dec-1880 – **John Webster** sold 2 ½ acres of land to **Robert Francis** for $1. The quit claim is recorded in volume 1 page 415 of the Newington land records.

Order 2
Paid a total of $37.25, **J.G. Stoddard** received $34.50 for services as a school visitor and $2.75 to **Mrs. J.G. Stoddard** for "returning births and deaths"

Order 5
Paid $ 20 to **J.S. Stoddard** for "special school appropriation"

Order 8
Paid a total of $24.95 to **L.W. Dunham** for the following; packing stone $8.75, medicine and wood for **A. Hills** $8.70, and lamps for **J.G. Wells** $7.50

Order 9
Paid **John R. Stoddard** $20 for services as Registrar

Order 12
Paid **T.R. Atwood** $20 for services as Registrar.

Order 14
Paid a total of $55.11 to **J.H. Fish** for supplying "coal and supplies" to the following people; **Mrs. Gilbert** $11.50, **Mrs. Squires** $11.60, **Mrs. Ramsey** $12, and **M. Applebee** $16.13. He was also paid; $1 for a lantern and $2.88 for "coal for Town Hall".

Order 16
Paid a total of $30.27 to **E. Kilbourne** for the following; $5.67 for certificates of burial and Town Hall repairs, and supplies for **A. Hills** $5.10, **M. Applebee** $6.50 and **Mrs. Ramsey** $13.

Order 17
Paid $23.75 to **J.E. Atwood** for; services as Assessor $20, assessor blanks $2.25, and service as Surveyor $1.50.

Order 18
Paid **A.D. Vorce** $22.50 for the care of **Mrs. Wm. Dee**.

Order 19
Paid out $279.45 to **Patrick Hoy**. This total was for; "breaking of snow banks" $3.25, spikes and planks for the new bridge near **William Applebee's** $16.80, rails, posts, nails and construction of same bridge $8.40, 1 plow share $1, and road account $250.

Order 20
Paid out a total of $12. Both **L.W. Camp** and **W.B. Dorman** received $6 each for their services on the Board of Relief.

Order 21
Paid **J.S. Kirkham** a total of $22.85 which included; registrar of vital statistics $17.35 and $5 for a right-of-way.

Order 22
C. Whaples was paid $10 for supplies and care of **Mrs. A. Whaples**.

Order 23
Paid $32.77 to **L. Wetherell** for the following; repairing of scraper $1.05, medicine and supplies for, **A. Hills** $13.72, **M. Applebee** $3.40, **Mrs. Ramsey** $1.20, and **Mrs. A. Whaples** $13.40.

Order 24
Paid $10 to **Mrs. Lucy E. Whaples** for attending **Mrs. A. Whaples** while sick.

Order 27
Paid **Patrick Hoy** $41 for "balance due on new road near Grace Church".

Order 32
L.W. Dunham was paid $10 for "cutting 5 cords of wood in cemetery".

Order 34
Paid $25 to **E. Kilbourne** for the following; supplies for, **Mrs. Ramsey** $13, **M. Applebee** $6.50, and **A. Hills** $1, digging a grave $3, reset a fence post $0.50, and clearing brush from the cemetery $1.

Order 36
Paid $5.25 to **Dr. L.V. Durand** for the medicine and care of **J. Clossen**.

Order 38
W.P. Davis was paid $15 for "rent for **Mrs. Waldo Gilbert** from Oct 1, 1879 to Apr 1, 1880"

Order 39
R. Welles was paid $25 for his service as a Selectman.

Order 43
Paid a total of $19 to **J.H. Fish** for the following; supplies for, **J. Clossen** $2, **Mrs. Ramsey** $0.98, **Mrs. Squires** $6, **M. Applebee** $6.75 and $3.35 for nails, lantern and a globe. The listed items actually total $19.08.

Order 51
Paid for $43.12 to **H. Luce** for supplying wood to **A. Hills** $3, **Applebee** $3 and $37.12 for oak plank for bridge.

Order 53
Paid out a total of $46.46 to **J. Deming** for the following; $10 for services as Assessor, supplies for; **A. Hills** $4.36, **Mrs. Ramsey** $0.60, **Mrs. Waldo Gilbert** $1.50 and $30 for bridge repair at new depot. Also included in this order was $7 paid to **Mrs. Porter Blinn** for the "attendance of **Mrs. A. Hills**" and $4 to **Mrs. S.A. Steele** for "attendance of **Mrs. A. Hills**".

Order 54
Dr. L.V. Durand was paid $12 for medical attendance on **Mrs. M. Applebee**.

Order 57

Paid $10 to **J.W. Woolley** for a coffin for **A. Hills**.

Order 58

Paid $12 to Hartford Hospital for "board of **M. McDermott**".

Order 64

E. Kilbourne received $25.65 for supplies for; **Mrs. Ramsey** $13, **M. Applebee** $6.50 and Town Hall $1.15 and $5 for mowing the burying ground.

Order 66

Paid **H. Griswold** $19.50 for supplies to **Mrs. A. Whaples**.

Order 67

Paid $8.75 to **S.H. Kilbourne** for "work at new bridge".

Order 69

Paid $5.10 to **M.L. Stoddard** for "posts, rails, and setting of same".

Order 73

E. Shelton received $6 for services on the Board of Relief.

Order 74

Paid $29.13 to **D.L. Robbins** for; service as Treasurer $25, stationary $0.75, and wood to **Mrs. A. Whaples** $3.38.

Order 75

Dr. A.S. Warner received $30.40 for medicine and attendance of **Mrs. A. Hills**.

Order 78

Paid a total of $40.99 to **T. Markley** for supplies to; **A. Hills** $1.30, **Mrs. Ramsey** $2, **Mrs. Squires** $6.84, and $4 for service as Selectman, $3.60 for nails and kerosene for bridge, $2.25 for stationary and stamps, and $20 as "salary per vote". [These items actually only total $39.99] Also included in this order is $1 to **R. Welles** for service as Selectman and $20 to **H.M. Robbins** for 9 ¾ days as selectman.

Order 81

Paid out $48.60 to **J.S. Kirkham** for the following; service as Town Clerk $19.10, making and recording of 16 liens $16, making rate book $7, cash paid for Town books $2.50, and enrolling military $4.

Bibliography

Ancestry.com. *Connecticut, Hale Collection of Cemetery Inscriptions and Newspaper Notices, 1629-1934* [database on-line]. Provo, UT, USA: Ancestry.com Operations, Inc., 2012.

Ancestry.com. *U.S. Federal Census - 1880 Schedules of Defective, Dependent, and Delinquent Classes* [database on-line]. Provo, UT, USA: Ancestry.com Operations, Inc., 2010.

Ancestry.com and The Church of Jesus Christ of Latter-day Saints. *1880 United States Federal Census* [database on-line]. Lehi, UT, USA: Ancestry.com Operations Inc, 2010.

Tillotson, Edward Sweetser. *Wethersfield Inscriptions: A Complete Record of the Inscriptions in the Five Burial Places in the Ancient Town of Wethersfield Including the Towns of Rocky Hill, Newington, and Beckley Quarter (in Berlin), also a Portion of the Inscription in the Oldest Cemetery in Glastonbury.* Hartford: William F.J. Boardman, 1899.

Town of Newington. *Land Records.* Newington Town Clerk's Office.

Town of Newington. *Newington Tax Levy 1880.* Newington Town Clerk's Office.

Town of Newington. *Selectmen Records Vol. 1, 1871 – 1980.* Newington Town Clerk's Office.

Town of Newington. *Town of Newington Town Meetings Vol. 1, 1871 – 1915.* Newington Town Clerk's Office.

Town of Newington. *Town Reports 1875 – 1908.* Newington Town Clerk's Office.

Welles, Roger (Ed.). *Early Annals of Newington, Comprising: The First Records Of The Newington Ecclesiastical Society, And Of The Congregational Church Connected Therewith; With Documents And Papers Relating To The Early History Of The Parish.* Hartford: Press Of The Case, Lockwood & Brainard Co., 1874.

Acknowledgments

An undertaking of this nature always requires the assistance and opinion of others.

I would like to thank the Newington Town Clerk and the staff there. They were (and are) always ready to lend a hand in finding the records that were needed to be reviewed. The knowledge of their records was immeasurably helpful. They are also very adept at interpreting the many various hand writing samples from the past.

The reference staff at the Lucy Robbins Welles Library in Newington always made themselves available to inquiries and always offered help and suggestions as needed.

Lee Ann your patience and encouragement is always appreciated as are your editorial comments and questions. You have helped me see a few of these types of projects through to the end. Thanks again.

Abbey who taught me about the Oxford Comma and is always available to add her own editorial comments when asked. She is a fine writer in her own right. Thank you.

www.ingramcontent.com/pod-product-compliance
Lightning Source LLC
Chambersburg PA
CBHW080338270326
41927CB00014B/3278